The Decline of the Novel

Other Books of Interest from St. Augustine's Press

Joseph Bottum, *The Second Spring*

Joseph Bottum, *The Fall & Other Poems*

Christopher Kaczor, *The Gospel of Happiness:*
How Secular Psychology Points to the Wisdom of Christian Practice

David Ramsay Steele, *The Mystery of Fascism*

James V. Schall, *On the Principles of Taxing Beer:*
And Other Brief Philosophical Essays

Promise Hsu, *China's Quest for Liberty: A Personal History of Freedom*

Rémi Brague, *The Anchors in the Heavens*

Rémi Brague, *Moderately Modern*

Josef Pieper, *Exercises in the Elements: Essays–Speeches–Notes*

Josef Pieper, *Traditional Truth, Poetry, Sacrament:*
For My Mother, on her 70th Birthday

Josef Pieper, *A Jouney to Point Omega: Autobiography from 1964*

Peter Kreeft, *Socrates' Children: The 100 Greatest Philosophers*

Peter Kreeft, *Ethics for Beginners: 52 "Big Ideas" from 32 Great Minds*

John von Heyking, *Comprehensive Judgment and Absolute Selflessness:*
Winston Churchill on Politics as Friendship

Alexandre Kojève, *The Concept, Time, and Discourse*

Barry Cooper, *Consciousness and Politics:*
From Analysis to Meditation in the Late Work of Eric Voegelin

James F. Pontuso, *Nature's Virtue*

Roger Scruton, *The Politics of Culture and Other Essays*

Roger Scruton, *The Meaning of Conservatism: Revised 3rd Edition*

Roger Scruton, *An Intelligent Person's Guide to Modern Culture*

Leon J. Podles, *Losing the Good Portion: Why Men Are Alienated from Christianity*

Gabriel Marcel, *The Invisible Threshold: Two Plays by Gabriel Marcel*

Stanley Rosen, *The Language of Love: An Interpretation of Plato's Phaedrus*

The Decline of the Novel

Joseph Bottum

St. Augustine's Press

South Bend, Indiana

Library of Congress Control Number: 2019951685

∞ The paper used in this publication meets the minimum
requirements of the American National Standard for Information Sciences –
Permanence of Paper for Printed Materials, ANSI Z39.48-1984.

St. Augustine's Press
www.staugustine.net

TABLE OF CONTENTS

CHAPTER 1 | THE WAY WE READ NOW

I

For almost three hundred years, the novel was a major art form, perhaps *the* major art form, of the modern world—the device by which, more than any other, we tried to explain ourselves to ourselves. Reading novels, we learned difference: undertaking unfamiliar journeys, experiencing alternate lives, seeing the world through unaccustomed lenses. At the same time, we learned similitude: the uniqueness of each self matched by the assertion of the shared fact that all human beings *are* interior selves and the characters in a novel *are* their readers, as those readers would be in a similar setting. (Or, at least, as they would want to be, told a story of the admirable, or as they hoped not to be, told a story of the repellent).

The old melodramatic roles of external figure—the hero, the villain, the coquette, the harlequin, the trickster—did not exactly go away. How could they? They are inscribed down in the deepest patterns of storytelling from which the novel emerged. *A boy met a girl. A stranger came to town. A man found himself a long, long way from home.* Like paths through the countryside, worn smooth by all the earlier travelers, there are established tracks that storytellers tend to follow. And that is so not just because they are familiar but because, more often than not, they really are the best ways to travel: the paths of least resistance; the tracks along which stories themselves want to go, shaped by the landscape of narrative.

Still, something new came into art during the culture's transition out of the Middle Ages, through the Renaissance and the Reformation, and into the modern age. We might call it the turn to the interior—meaning, in part, an increasing cultural agreement that domestic life and domestic drama are real. They are not merely incidental, not merely the minor activities necessary to keep body and soul together while we play out our real lives of illustrative moral action on the world's public stage.

Given the traditionally non-public roles of women, we shouldn't be surprised that so many of the new books written with these new interests were by female authors. But innumerable novels were written by male authors as well, and even in those books we can sense something like a reversal. It could sometimes seem, in novels, as though public life is what now appeared a little vague, a little unimportant—the things people do to make enough money that they can afford to go home and live their real lives. It's not much of an exaggeration to say that none of the defining novels of the eighteenth and nineteenth centuries, the towering monoliths that established the art form, offered readers a compelling narrative of the work people actually perform in money-making business. Nor is it much of an exaggeration to say that none of them conveyed a good sense of the high-stakes drama of commerce, however much the modern age was shaped by the economic changes that created bourgeois commercial life.

Try as he might in *The Way We Live Now* (1875), a novel of outrage at London's stock-jobbing corruption, even an author as interested in money as Anthony Trollope cannot quite convince us that what his businessmen do in their day-to-day work is as morally and emotionally weighty—as novelistically interesting—as what they do in private. In *The Prime Minister* (1876), the small but brutal passage in which the bankrupt Ferdinand Lopez contemptuously dismisses the mistress he can no longer afford, like the more extended scene in which he prepares to throw himself in front of a train, is far more powerful and fraught than any of the vague descriptions offered by Trollope for what Lopez actually does as a financial speculator. To find much sense of the adventure of making money we have to wait for a novel as late as, perhaps, *The Card* (1911), an enjoyable if minor Edwardian comedy by Arnold Bennett. (This is to set aside, as perhaps we shouldn't, such grim, would-be *Poor Richard's* fables as the 1868 *Ragged Dick*, the first of Horatio Alger's rags-to-riches bestsellers for American boys. Even those books, however, show a curious impatience with making money. The typical Alger tale ends up rewarding its thrifty, hard-working boy hero with a sudden and implausible windfall about two-thirds of the way through, just to hurry the story along.)

In an illuminating footnote to his 2004 translation of Genesis, the literary critic Robert Alter points out how unexpectedly domestic is the story of Sarah, Hagar, and Abraham: the drama of the barren Sarah's offering her handmaiden to her husband, her subsequent jealousy when Hagar succeeds at becoming pregnant, her laughing (and then denying that she had laughed) at the prophecy that she would bear a child in old age. Is it any wonder that Sarah is a rare woman in the Old Testament whose age at her death is given? Even in the Bible's highly compressed way of telling stories, she emerges as an emotionally rich character, approaching even Joseph and David, the most psychologically complete biblical figures.

Another reason for noticing the story, however, is the rareness of the domestic drama it presents. Other ancient possibilities tend to falter when we come to think about them. Penelope is spinning not so much private life as politics in the domestic settings of her life in the *Odyssey*, Dido is laying down the markers of history in the *Aeneid*, and the goddess Ishtar is performing something at the level of theogony with her anger in *Gilgamesh*. But for all Sarah's historical and theological consequence, her figure is shown in these scenes from Genesis simply doing domestic life: its tragedies, its joys, its furies, its contentments. Ancient literature does not give us many such moments.

Recognizing that lack, we can understand why the flood of the modern novel felt so new to readers in the eighteenth and nineteenth centuries. In, say, Flaubert's delicate notice of the vaginal bruising that poor, idiotic Emma Bovary feels after relentless trysts with her domineering lover Rodolphe, we see not just a new sexual explicitness (however obliquely written) and not just the kind of close observation that would become almost the definition of realistic narration after Flaubert's 1857 triumph of *Madame Bovary*. We see, as well, that modern novels had entered the personal and private spheres in ways unimagined by any previous art.

And yet, when we speak of the turn to the interior with the modern novel, we mean more than just precisely observed details and scenes of domestic life. We also mean something for which those personal details and domestic scenes are often symbolic representations. The art form of the novel gave us a fascination with the interior self, its emotions and its reasonings, greater and more insistent than anything the world had ever known before.

This modern sense of self could be traced along the line of high philosophy, from Descartes through Rousseau and down to Immanuel Kant (noticing, for example, that the epistemological problem of the self, the question of how we know, received a phrasing with which we still speak of

3

it in Kant's use of the distinction between *objectivity* and *subjectivity*). Or we could follow the struggles of the modern self through the economics of emerging capitalism—analyzed, from Marx on, in terms of the dissociation of workers from the work they do. Perhaps most tellingly, we could turn to foundational Protestant theology, from Martin Luther to Jonathan Edwards, finding a root of the modern self in the Reformation's profound focusing of religious attention on the salvation and sanctification of the individual soul.

None of these ways of thinking about the modern self excludes the others. The different streams of modernity had what the sociologist Max Weber called an "elective affinity," and they all ended up joining to make a great, unstoppable river. Together they formed in us "the punctual self," as Charles Taylor has dubbed it in one of his philosophical studies of modern history: To be modern is to experience the mind itself as a kind of exteriority; we see our desires and thoughts as though they were objective elements that we can catalogue, understand, and explain—and thereby perhaps manipulate and change.

Even to begin describing all the ways in which this new sense of self emerged in modernity would consume dozens of chapters, a good number of them merely trailing after Taylor's sprawling, multi-track masterpieces of *Sources of the Self* (1989) and *A Secular Age* (2007). But there is, I think, a shorter path toward understanding the effect of that modern self, and we find it by paging through the history of the modern novel. Novels became central to the culture in part because their narratives were the only available art form spacious enough for all the details authors needed if they were to draw what was increasingly seen as realistic pictures of their characters. That kind of literary space just doesn't exist in lyrical poetry, despite the deep personal emotion the Romantics would use that poetry to express.

For that matter, the novel developed into a crucial art because it was one of the key ways in which people learned to have modern selves. Yes, those book-length stories aimed, as every art aims, to entertain and instruct. But how did they entertain, and what did they instruct? From the eighteenth-century's Samuel Richardson on, novels populated their stories with interior selves, and they taught readers to find fascinating the details of those selves—aiding the development (and enforcing the reality) of the punctual self. With its new technologies of printing, binding, and distributing books, the modern age made the novel possible as a widespread cultural artifact. And the novel returned the compliment, teaching its readers how they should understand themselves in the new age.

Most of all, the novel grew into a great art form because it promised something more than detailed stories of modern selves. Along the way, the culture generally came to believe that the art was doing significant cultural work. These books were not simply giving us entertaining pictures of the ways we think of ourselves. They were describing, with increasing urgency, what seemed the crisis of those modern selves. And at their highest and most serious level, they were offering solutions to the crisis.

Here we reach the vital point, the reason for stepping back to take a look at the flow of literature—for we need a way to understand our cultural history, a way of understanding ourselves and how we live now. The sad truth is that the novel just isn't what it used to be. It doesn't occupy the same cultural high ground, and it doesn't typically feel to readers like much of a practical device for addressing serious problems. Over the past few decades, we have experienced a growing disbelief in the power of what Western culture once routinely understood as its most illuminating art, and something disturbing is revealed by this breakdown of the old agreement between readers and writers that novels *matter*.

The decline of the novel's prestige reflects and confirms a genuine cultural crisis. This is not just the old crisis of the self, but a new crisis born of the culture's increasing failure of intellectual nerve and terminal doubt about its own progress. We have to believe in a culture to employ that culture's art: to be much entertained by it, and to be much instructed.

II

Of course I know, as you know, any number of dedicated novel-readers today. But I do not know—and I suspect you do not know—many who still read novels in the older senses: novel-reading as a necessary part of participation in public life, akin to (and more important than) the news. Or novel-reading as the great hunt for insight into the human condition, akin to (or, at least, providing the raw material for) serious intellectual analysis of ethics, political theory, and psychology. Or novel-reading as the chance to observe authors performing heroic acts of cultural hygiene, akin to protest and public oratory. I do not know—and suspect you do not know—many readers who still believe that novels are significant not just as a story-reading hobby, not just as a nostalgic indulgence, not just as wonderful genre-fiction escapes into mysteries, thrillers, and sci-fi worlds, but as the thing itself: our deepest, truest, and most vital art. They do not know novels, in other words, as the most profound expressions of psychological, sociological, and existential truths. Novels as the source of examples from which those trailing intellectual disciplines must draw.

And even if, by chance, we are acquainted with such readers, they no longer have the ear of the general culture. No one feels bad anymore for not reading novels. No one feels it important to mouth the old, middlebrow pieties about the need for the Great American Novel or the necessity to fill the space once occupied by the likes of Charles Dickens, or Ernest Hemingway, or Saul Bellow.

Art forms are not immortal or incapable of collapse when their social foundations shift. Think, for example, of Latin elegy. What little we possess of the remains of Old Latin gives us no real sense of the native poetry of the language; it might have had the stress-base or even the rhyme to which Late Ecclesial Latin would turn in the Goliards and Thomas Aquinas's great medieval hymns-as-marching-songs. Regardless, in the rise of Rome from hilltop village to Mediterranean power, Old Latin verse was swept away by the Romans' joyous discovery of Greek forms, and Latin poetry would soon approach Greek in the power and subtlety of its quantitative syllable-length meter.

The Roman poets, in other words, remade their language with a Greek poetics, and in the late Republic and early Empire the elegy was a dominant and natural form of Latin poetry—until suddenly it wasn't. It wasn't even an important art form anymore. Why did the Romans essentially abandon elegy for other (still usually Greek) forms as the Empire progressed? A half-dozen explanations could be cobbled up, but the point is that the Romans did generally move away from the form as a serious part of their poetry. An art form can die, even after something like the extraordinary two-hundred-year run of Latin's elegiac couplet from Ennius (born around 239 B.C.) to Ovid (who died in A.D. 17).

Or think of the epic, which Aristotle names in the *Poetics* as the highest and most worthy of arts. What can we add, after Homer, Virgil, and Dante?

As he sweeps through the history of English verse in his *Lives of the English Poets*, Samuel Johnson jokes that one of the reactions to the 1667 *Paradise Lost* wasn't surprise that John Milton had written an epic, but surprise that *anyone* could write a successful epic at that late date. (And even then, Johnson famously concluded, *"Paradise Lost* is one of the books which the reader admires and puts down, and forgets to take up again. None ever wished it longer than it is.")

Think, for that matter, of English poetry in general—for poetry would somehow cease to be a major part of broad public discourse in America by (at the latest) the deaths of the poets W.H. Auden and Robert Lowell in the 1970s. Who now feels they must read new poetry to be a literate person aware of the strong tides of culture? Many readers still follow the publication of new poetry; poetry may even be undergoing something of a revival after its 1990s nadir. But few readers today are able to take that poetry as readers could have taken it around 1959—that is, poetry reading as a public act, an inescapable requirement for a public life in the intellectual realm.

For an art to have this kind of public power requires a general agreement between artists and audience about the ready capacity of that art to entertain and instruct. The shapes and rules of that agreement will need some exploration, as we think about the novel as an art form. But for now, we might merely say that if the novel no longer possesses a general public agreement about its significance, well, so be it. Art forms rise and art forms fall, and the world moves on.

In the twentieth century, recording technology allowed the art of song lyrics to assume a larger place in our lives than ever before. The invention of film offered wildly new ways to present narratives. Television reestablished open-ended serial storytelling, as though Samuel Richardson had somehow been reborn in an alien age. The creation of the computer game and the rise of the Internet gave us many other forms of excitement. Narrative art is still made, in other words. Stories are still told in other forms, even while old-fashioned novels are still written for those who want them in their now more cloistered sense.

Along the way, English-language genre fiction has blossomed into a startling new maturity. Popular biography has grown again into an accepted device for conveying some of lessons the novel once delivered—as has popularly presented sociology, of the kind once typified by, for example,

7

William H. Whyte's *The Organization Man* (1956). In almost any other moment of modern times, wouldn't we have received in a novel, instead of a collection of nonfiction essays, something like David Brooks's smart and satirical observations of American social class in *Bobos in Paradise* (2000)? Perhaps not. From Jonathan Swift and Benjamin Franklin to Thorstein Veblen and H.L. Mencken, social satire has arrived often enough in the guise of nonfiction. But Brooks is an heir to the "New Journalism" of the 1960s and 1970s, which used techniques of novel-writing to do essay-length reporting. Both *Bobos in Paradise* and his later *The Social Animal* (2011) are, in their different ways, something like William Dean Howells's novel, *The Rise of Silas Lapham*, retold as popular sociology.

All this says little of the ways we are, in this online age, inundated with the text of news aggregators, blogs, phone apps, and all the rest of the computerized experience. We hardly lack for prose.

Still, we should not let the decline of the novel from its once-dominant place pass unnoticed. In many of its old cultural functions, the novel is moribund—and this fact tells us something about the condition of the culture in which the novel once flourished. The novel really was the canary in the coal mine, to use that hackneyed image, and its gasping for breath now signals a kind of failure of nerve, an end of confidence, about the past values and future goals of what conceived itself as Western culture. If we can't do our fundamental art work well anymore, if the culturally central agreement between artist and audience has decayed, then the signs of a weakened, diffident, and timid culture are written in the dust on the unread books of our library shelves.

In my 2014 book, *An Anxious Age*, I argued that the greatest (and yet mostly unremarked) sociological change in America over the past fifty years is the collapse of the Mainline Protestant churches—from somewhere around 50 percent of Americans in 1965 to under 10 percent today. This collapse removed a central support of American identity, I argued. Though Jews and Catholics (like me) and others were welcomed, on and off, through the history of the United States, we understood that we lived in what was in its essence a Protestant nation. The history of the dominant churches, of what would come to be called the Mainline, was the cultural Mississippi pouring through the center of the nation and its self-understanding.

When that great wellspring dried up—for reasons too myriad and complex to lay out again here in this small study of the novel as an art form—a sense of the old culture gasped for breath and died in the hard-baked mud of a dead river. Even more problematic, I argued, the collapse of the Mainline Protestant churches set loose social demons that had once been corralled and bridled by those churches. They were free to enter politics, for example. And thus, when we think that our ordinary political opponents are not merely mistaken but actually evil, we have not so much politicized religion as religionized politics. Concepts that once seemed theological now appear political.

My argument in *An Anxious Age* may convince readers, or it may not. Certainly a study of the novel as an art form does not stand or fall on the success of the *Anxious Age* thesis. The temporal progression of ideas is not the same as the logical progression, so it should not matter what prior ideas prompted later ideas. Nonetheless, it may bear mentioning that I first conceived of this book on the decline of the novel as a particular application and case-study of the decline of magisterial Protestantism as central to the culture of the United States and northwestern Europe. As the theological foundations decayed, so did the cultural institutions built on those foundations. And that includes the arts of the civilization that once ranked the novel among its most important forms.

As it happens, the novel—from its High Victorian peak through its full modernist ambition—was often engaged in sour, brutal, and unrelenting criticism of the culture in which it appeared. But that criticism of the culture's present proceeded from a curious lack of criticism about the possibilities of the culture's future. The novel generally contained what we might call a confident critique, born from an assumption of strength and worthiness—born, most of all, from an assumption of access to the great truths of morality and the structures of the universe by which we could find a guide.

In other words, the sins of Western culture could be criticized in the highest tones of moral outrage, because few readers doubted that Western culture was called to something higher. Our failures could be mocked with the most unremitting and vicious comedy because those failures were perceived as actually *failures*, as authors and their readers alike knew. Confidence in the general frame of culture allowed a useful, socially advancing complaint about the ill-fit and corrupt elements held within that frame.

The novel was a device for understanding and improving ourselves within an accepted cultural setting of belief in the possibility of understanding and improvement. And when we turned, as many artists did, to criticism of the setting itself—turned, as many artists did, to a desire to smash the frame—the novel in its social aspect ceased to be as useful as it had once seemed.

All this is testimony, I think, to the current problem of culture's lack of belief in itself, derived from the fading of a temporal horizon. We walk with our heads down. History appears to have no discernable aim, and culture no visible end. Without a sense of the old goals and reasons—a sense of the good achieved, understood as progress—all that remains are the crimes the culture committed in the past to get where it is now. Uncompensated by achievement, unexplained by purpose, these unameliorated sins must seem overwhelming: the very definition of the culture. For that matter, without a sense of the old goals and reasons, why should we strain for the future? Why, indeed, should we write or even read book-length fiction for insight into the directions of the culture and the self?

And so, generally speaking, we don't bother much with those books anymore. We don't teach them in college in any systematic way. We don't expect that even the educated will have a sure sense of the form. The local libraries have given up on acting as repositories of literary history, moving a few copies of Dickens and Hemingway to the "Young Adults" section and pulping the rest. Although their positions in universities derive from the prestige that literature once possessed, literary scholars now study, for example, the dated pornography of naughty French postcards with the same tools and the same enthusiasms they once used for the novel; the typical English department in the United States has more professors with a specialty or subspecialty in movies than in anything else.

The novel didn't fail us. We failed the novel.

III

Except, of course, that we didn't. Not exactly. To a real extent, the eventual failure of nerve was foretold in the first moments of the modern age—in the first emergence of the modern self and the first printing of a modern novel. Despite the long tradition of critics who interpret modern literary history as a tale of increasing secularization, I see the cultural purpose of writing and reading novels as genuinely religious, down at the root. The rise of the art form and its subsequent flowering are not what show us the decay of religious belief in Western culture. If anything, it is the current decline of the novel that suggests a kind of impersonal secularization, with the culture rooting out the last unconscious elements of the cultural Christendom that had maintained the generally shared confidence about its progress.

As for that religious sense of these books, perhaps we can think of it this way: In some of its most serious purposes, the novel as an art form aimed at re-enchantment. It hungered to find or create with its stories a kind of glow to the objects of the world, a thickness of essential meaning in realities that had been rendered down to nothing more than thin existence by the modern world's turn to technological science, bureaucratic government, and commercial economics. If the natural world is imagined by modernity as empty of purpose, then the hunt for nature's importance is *supernatural*, by definition. If the physical order is defined by its sheer scientifically measured presence, its brute facticity, then the search for meaning in the physical order is necessarily *metaphysical*. And if the secular realm is understood as merely arbitrary social arrangements enforced by the powerful, then the attempt to uncover social value must prove to be *religious*.

The mode of that novelistic religiousness proves, in hindsight, to have been quite Protestant, significantly formed by the Reformation's part in the cultural turn out of the medieval and into the modern. We can see it, for example, in the differences between Cervantes's *Don Quixote* from Catholic Spain in 1605 and Samuel Richardson's *Clarissa* from Protestant England in 1748. And yet, before we get to a closer reading of particular works, we should lay out briefly a description of the modern art form—not exactly sketching the argument of the following pages, but noting the arc of the story we need to have in mind as we read our way through the history of modern fiction.

The story starts with the art's religious roots. The modern novel had any number of ancestors, back through the history of writing, but it came squalling to birth in England in the eighteenth century and was wrapped in very Protestant clothing. The novel came into being to present the Protestant story of the individual soul as it strove to understand its salvation and achieve its sanctification, illustrated by the parallel journey of the new-style characters, with their well-furnished interiors, as they wandered through their adventures in the exterior world.

As modernity progressed, however, the thick inner world of the self increasingly came to seem ill-matched with the impoverished outer world, stripped of all the old enchantment that had made exterior objects seem meaningful and important, significant in themselves. This is what we mean by *the crisis of the self*: Why does anything matter, what could be important, if meaning is invented, coming *from* the self rather *to* the self? The novel—already running down parallel tracks of interior and exterior life thanks to its Protestant origin—was uniquely positioned as an art form to present a vivid picture of that crisis.

And, indeed, it was able to do something more than just present the crisis of the self. The novel was uniquely positioned to attempt to solve that crisis, as well. The novel was an opportunity for artists to assume the role of demiurges, filling their fictional worlds with meaning, re-enchanting the exterior setting in which their characters move, and thereby showing readers how to live well in modern times by uncovering connections between the self and the self's environment at any given moment in the historical progress of the culture.

Of course, to do so required a kind of confidence in the power of the artist, an agreement between authors and readers that the novel was doing important cultural work. Moreover, it required confidence in the progress of modernity and the aims of Western civilization. It depended on the belief both that we were going somewhere as a culture and that history had a goal, a horizon toward which modern times were moving.

Both of these confidences were the fruit of a vague but generally shared sense of culture, itself deeply influenced by the Reformation—a sort of Christian mood without much doctrinal content, a Protestantism of the Air, breathed even by those who were not Protestants. If the existence of the modern novel was influenced by the Reformation, born in confidently Protestant territory, so modernity itself was formed and with the Reformation as one of the key cultural changes that created it. Modern developments traceable to Protestantism thus provided novels both their birth as accounts of the new modern self and the cultural mood of progress that made them seem important—the cultural mood that lent those novels the power of their moral outrage, their increasingly high seriousness, and their life-changing effect.

From the eighteenth century through the twentieth, authors produced book-length fiction unlike anything the world had ever read, and they did it because the civilization *needed* them to do so. It rewarded them for doing so, too.

CHAPTER 2 | DIGGING FOR THE ROOT

I

So, here's a proposition. The novel was an art form—*the* art form—of the modern Protestant West, and as the main strength of established Protestant Christendom began to fail in Europe and the United States in recent decades, so did the cultural importance of the novel.

The proposition begins to unravel as soon as we offer it, of course. By the time we are done listing all the demurrals, adjustments, and trimmings, little seems left of the notion that the novel is an artifact of the Protestant West.

Little, however. Not *nothing*. The claim about the Protestant inflections of the novel is not intended here as exclusive. If modern times elected the novel as a significant art form, a central cultural expression, that does not necessarily imply some reductionist claim that other cultures and other ages and other authors were incapable of writing extended prose fictions. In truth, our exploration of the novel in the Protestant cultures of the modern world may end up telling us more about modernity and Protestant culture than it tells us about the novel.

Still, it's hardly a new thesis that the novel exploded out of eighteenth-century England to become a dominant art form of Western culture. In 1957, the literary critic Ian Watt published a much-discussed work called *The Rise of the Novel*, which claimed exactly that. Among academics, Watt is rather casually dismissed these days; certainly his work was significant back in the late 1950s, they might say in distant praise, but it valorizes male British authors, fails to appreciate the truly radical impulses suppressed by all organs of culture (including the publishers of novels), and implies that literature can be judged aesthetically beyond the determinations of power in social politics.

All of which is a little odd as a dismissal of Watt, for *The Rise of the Novel* was intent on finding solidly progressive and secularizing reasons for the rise of the novel. Watt looked, as a good socialist might, at economics, particularly the economics of book publishing. And he insisted, as a good rationalist might, on the scientific and industrial changes of society after the Middle Ages and the new understanding of the self as defined by the early modern philosophers, from Descartes to Locke.

What he did not much mention is the singular religious root of it all. Aware of the multiplicities of Protestantism, in all the variety of its post-Reformation sects in Great Britain, Watt nonetheless left unspoken the *unities* of Protestantism: the central current of manners and morals that Protestantism had created by the time it had reached its full cultural victory over Catholicism in England in the eighteenth century. This general Protestantism was, in a sense, too big for Watt to see—the received setting and given condition of the fiction. It was the *secret de Polichinelle* of the English novelists, the thing no one bothers to mention because they assume that everyone already knows it. And for too many subsequent literary critics, it became simply unknowable, hidden by their sure and certain faith in the novel as the mirror (or even the motor) of secularization.

Besides, we have two pieces of the puzzle that Watt did not, two further data points to use in modifying his thesis as we trace the history of the novel: the astonishing collapse of Mainline Protestantism in recent decades, and the simultaneous decay of the novel's central place in the culture. Even after all the necessary caveats and qualifications are registered, the notion of the modern novel's Protestant essence won't disappear—for *something* in the confident precincts of Western culture really did latch onto extended prose fiction in the eighteenth century, and it wouldn't let go as the centuries rolled by.

Yes, there was poetry and a flowering of music through those long years. Painting, sculpture, dance: all the outpouring of European art from the Renaissance on. Nonetheless, for nearly three centuries, the West increasingly took the novel as the art form most central to its cultural self-awareness as the artistic device by which the culture attempted some of its most serious attempts at self-understanding. And the form of that device was developed to explain and solve particularly Protestant problems of the self in modern times.

II

To get to a conclusion like that, we have to determine what we mean by the novel—the Novel with a capital *N*; the novel as an art form. And that proves exceedingly difficult. No one has any compelling idea of what unites *The Manuscript Found in Saragossa*, *Fanny Hill*, *Notes from Underground*, *My Ántonia*, *Nausea*, and *Midnight's Children* as a single type of writing. No one has any serious notion of what could possibly make the English writers Thomas Love Peacock, Ann Radcliffe, William Harrison Ainsworth, A.A. Milne, Daphne du Maurier, and Anthony Powell a single kind of author, even though we say that they all wrote novels.

Consider just this example: America has never had a strong tradition of political literature. The United States, in fact, has always tended toward apolitical or even *anti*-political fiction. The nation's enduring literary characters don't typically stump for office among their fellow citizens; they light out for the territory, or take to sea to hunt great whales, or buy million-dollar houses with huge balloon payments they don't know how the hell they can ever pay. We have a literature of eccentrics too peculiar, too busy, or too self-involved to notice politics, from Edgar Allan Poe's Arthur Gordon Pym and Sarah Orne Jewett's Mrs. Todd to Saul Bellow's Henderson the Rain King and John Kennedy Toole's Ignatius J. Reilly.

Even when those characters live public lives, they somehow sense that it isn't all they're meant for. Every American is conflicted in the same way, as an insurance agent in an Arthur Miller play observes: Any good, solid, middle-class American male is "a fourteen-room house—in the bedroom he's asleep with his intelligent wife, in the living-room he's rolling around with some bare-ass girl, in the library he's paying his taxes, in the yard he's raising tomatoes, and in the cellar he's making a bomb to blow it all up."

Political Britain may be enjoyed by Americans when they read, say, Anthony Trollope's parliamentary novels, but those same American readers would find it hard to retell *Phineas Redux* (1874) with an American setting. The streetwalkers of Emile Zola's France and the merchants of Thomas Mann's Germany have a surer grasp of politics than do the actual politicians in classic American fiction. After we've nodded toward Ward Just's deliberate attempts to make political fiction in the United States (capped by his What-do-Cold-Warriors-do-after-the-Cold-War? novel *Echo House* in 1997), the list of great American political fiction quickly dwindles down to such works as Henry Adams's awkward *Democracy* from 1880, Edwin O'Connor's Irish-American *The Last Hurrah* from 1956, and Allen Drury's journalistic *Advise and Consent*, winner of the Pulitzer Prize in 1959.

Still—and here's the point—even those mostly failed attempts to do politics in American fiction are still *novels*. Drury was not what anyone in the 1950s would have called the nation's best writer. The man had a prose so tedious it could barely plod to the corner store for a quart of milk without taking an hour over it. But if we do not count *Advise and Consent* as a genuine novel, then we have a truncated and unhelpful notion of the form. Meanwhile, we have to include somewhere in our capacious genre everything from Robert Bloch's *Psycho* to Terry Southern's *The Magic Christian*, together with Mordecai Richler's *The Apprenticeship of Duddy Kravitz* (from the small world of Jewish Canada) and Muriel Spark's *Memento Mori* (from the almost as small world of Catholic England)—all four of which were published the same year as Drury's sluggish classic.

Are we then forced back to the broad category of the novel as simply as an extended piece of fiction? If so, the literary history of humankind gives us novels long before eighteenth-century England came to be. Perhaps we can set aside the epic myth-tellings of the ancient world—*Gilgamesh*, the *Iliad*, the *Ramayana*, and all the rest—since they lack, we typically suppose, the self-conscious invention and falsity, the knowing fictitiousness, that we mean by the word *fiction*. And perhaps we can set aside works from the Latin *Aeneid* to the Old English *Beowulf* by holding a general insistence on prose (while admitting the modern verse novel as a specialty item in the canon, from Alexander Pushkin's 1831 *Eugene Onegin* to Vikram Seth's 1986 *The Golden Gate*).

Still, what are we to call the extended prose narratives of the ancient world—with the Romans giving us Petronius' *Satyricon* in the first century and Apuleius' *Golden Ass* in the second? What about Murasaki Shikibu's *Tale of Genji* (c. 1020) in Japan? What about the Chinese *Romance of the Three Kingdoms* (c. 1500)? If the novel is a modern, Protestant-inflected thing, then we are left without much of a category for Longus' second-century Greek *Daphnis and Chloe*, the seventh-century Sanskrit *Dashaku-maracharita*, and Thomas Malory's 1470s compilation of medieval romances, *Le Morte d'Arthur*—along with such seventeenth-century work as Marie de La Fayette's *The Princess of Clèves* and Miguel Cervantes's *Don Quixote*.

But it's exactly there, with a mention of the 1605 *Don Quixote*, that we begin to sense a change in those extended stories, a new and different world emerging, and Cervantes's work is always cited in this context as the first widely read book of fiction to be taken as modern. Before *Don Quixote*, we have novels with a sort of asterisk. Nod toward them as politely and judiciously as you want, they are nonetheless novels mostly by courtesy of their being works of extended prose fiction. After *Don Quixote*, we begin to have novels in the strictest sense anyone could want to give the word: book-length modern stories with a sense of spiritual development over the plot's timeline, characters who have interior selves, a drive toward artistic unity, and an ambition for the book to be revelatory commentary on the human condition.

The history of literature is never tidy. For all that the novel is an art form produced by ostensible heroes, the novelist understood as solitary genius, every breakthrough in some aspect of the form proves to have predecessors—unsuccessful or unrecognized or unfocused attempts to achieve the new effect before authors and audience were ready to accept it. One could find this fact, as we have, in the awkwardness of defining the novel as the art form of a particular era. Or one could find it in the question of what to do with Boccaccio, who predates Cervantes by 250 years. Indeed, we get the word *novel* from the Italian *novella*, which means *new*—the new style of shorter tales that the influential Boccaccio wrote in the *Decameron*.

For that matter, how are we to take *Gargantua and Pantagruel*, which Rabelais began publishing in France seventy years before *Don Quixote* appeared? In 2007, the Czech novelist Milan Kundera took to the pages of the *New Yorker* to insist that Rabelais belongs with Cervantes, and probably above him, as "the founder of an entire art, the art of the novel."

Most readers will understand what Kundera means. *Gargantua and Pantagruel* is a sprawling mess, true enough—a large loose baggy monster of a book, to use the phrase with which Henry James described Thackeray's *The Newcomes* (1855), Dumas's *The Three Musketeers* (1844), and Tolstoy's *War and Peace* (1869). What are these monsters attempting, artistically, "with their queer elements of the accidental and the arbitrary"?

In James's disparaging line we can hear the High Victorian goal of making the novel a tight and self-complete work of great art, as unified as a Beethoven symphony: symbol, plot, character, and diction all moving toward a single end. Novelists should seek "an absolutely premeditated art," James insisted. Monstrously baggy novels may have life, but it is life "as waste," artistic life "sacrificed and thereby prevented from 'counting.'" We need "the artist, the divine explanatory genius, who will come to our aid"—employing "a deep-breathing economy and an organic form," to arrive at a work of art with "complete pictorial fusion."

It seems almost needless to say that Rabelais had no such Henry James-like ambitions, which tends to weaken Kundera's claiming of *Gargantua and Pantagruel* as the foundation of the modern novel. In his seminal 1965 study of the book, Mikhail Bakhtin identified the mad festival of *Gargantua and Pantagruel* as entirely *premodern*: a definitively Renaissance work by a bawdy Christian humanist very much in the line of Erasmus. And in this, I think, we have to side with Bakhtin. Only the thinnest account of Western literature would dismiss *Gargantua and Pantagruel* as merely a cul-de-sac and a curiosity. Nevertheless, there is a discernable difference between Cervantes and Rabelais, just as there is a difference between Cervantes and Boccaccio, for *Don Quixote* presents us with something new and distinct in the post-classical West—that is, something both more modern and more of what we recognize as a novel than anything that had come before.

I do not wish to hide the evaluation of Cervantes toward which I'm aiming. Hearing an attempt to dismiss *Don Quixote* as incidental to the history of the modern novel, we should leap to the book's defense. *This* is where the novel first emerges; *this* is one of the few truly great works of world literature, and without it we do not have much of what follows: No Cervantes, no Dickens. At the same time, hearing an attempt to claim *Don Quixote* as the very definition of the modern novel, we should shy a little. It's a long, improbable path from Cervantes's La Mancha to Mrs. Gaskell's *Cranford*, and the possibilities of books as diverse as *Daniel Deronda, Là-bas, Portrait of the Artist as a Young Man*, and *The Glass Bead Game* are not easily discerned in the pages of *Don Quixote*.

Similarly, the eighteenth-century English works of Defoe, Richardson, and Fielding—the figures named as central by Ian Watt in his study of the emerging novel—are not derived from *Don Quixote* quite as easily as literary histories often assume. In *Cervantes, the Novel, and the New World* (2000), the critic Diana de Armas Wilson attacks Watt as a narrow-minded British nationalist and quite possibly an anti-Hispanic racist for undervaluing Cervantes in his effort "to install Daniel Defoe as 'the first key figure in the rise of the novel'"—the key figure not merely in the rise of the English novel but in the rise of the novel itself as a modern art form.

19

But surely we can distinguish Cervantes and Defoe without being accused of chauvinism and bigotry, for the two authors are writing different books and aiming at different ends. Something has changed between Cervantes and Defoe. Something separates the Catholic Spain of 1605 in which *Don Quixote* appears from the Protestant England of 1719 in which *Robinson Crusoe* is published. Something has allowed the inner life of the hero to appear on the page. And, I want to claim, those *somethings* involve the Protestant presentation of the spiritual journey of the main character as a unique self—together with the English novel's determination to provide alternate lives for the reader to experience vicariously and the confident sense of modernity as an age defined by more than its rebellion against the medieval past.

However modern *Don Quixote* seems when compared with the *Decameron* or *Gargantua and Pantagruel*, Cervantes's work can also feel unmodern to readers now. Think, for example, of how new characters suddenly appear, chance-met along the hero's journey, and promptly begin telling chapter-length stories. They are barely related interpolations that serve mostly to bulk up the text with something interesting. This picaresque device will last until at least Dickens's 1839 *Nicholas Nickleby*, but the Victorian age quickly thereafter grew too embarrassed to use it much. The rise of magazines allowed such smaller tales to take clearer shape within an author-and-reader agreement about the genre of short stories, and the interpolated tale came to seem something like an admission of failure: an acknowledgement that the author had not succeeded at finding the unified work of art that defined the High Victorian novel, from *Jane Eyre* to *The Wings of the Dove*.

Think, too, of the curious meta-fictional comedy of the second part of *Don Quixote* (with the characters portrayed as having read the first part of the novel that created them)—from which one could point out a different direction the central current of the art form might have taken. In fact, some novels *did* flow down that rival streambed, starting with the classic self-referential, Möbius-strip comedy of Laurence Sterne's 1759 *Tristram Shandy* (by an author who often refers to Rabelais, in confirmation of our sense of an alternate history the novel could have followed).

In other words, the influence of Cervantes was certainly present in the beginning: Interest in the author's work helped begin the eighteenth-century run of British picaresques and thereby contributed greatly to the establishment of the novel as a ready form of art in the English language. In the 1850 *David Copperfield*, Dickens's clearest signal that he was leaving the picaresque for the unified art work of the Victorian novel, the eponymous hero pauses to name the books he read when he was young—and they are all the spawn of Cervantes: *Gil Blas*, Tobias Smollett's stories of *Roderick Random*, *Peregrine Pickle*, and *Humphrey Clinker*. Even *Tom Jones*, *The Vicar of Wakefield*, and *Robinson Crusoe*, in the way David describes reading them as imaginary (and sexually innocent) journeys fulfilling the child's desperate desire to escape. Oppressed by his mother's new husband, the young David retreats to reading—"reading as if for life," in Dickens's beautiful phrase— in the picaresque books that are his only inheritance from his father. But even while Dickens reveals the influence of *Don Quixote* on the early years of the modern novel, Cervantes's meta-fictional play may actually prove to have had a greater effect on the final years of the modern novel, a key element in the creation of postmodern fiction.

Interestingly, to readers trained by the success of the English novel from Jane Austen to Virginia Woolf, *Don Quixote* will seem least modern in precisely the feature that leads historians to declare it modern: its turn against the failures and oddities of late medieval culture. The book's primary literary device is mockery—and thus a kind of acknowledgment—of its predecessors in the proto-novels of the heroic late-medieval Romances and such Pastorals as Sannazaro's 1480 poetic *Arcadia* and Montemayor's 1559 prose *Diana*.

Not all the world was necessarily pleased. One could make the case that *Richard II* is a deeper literary analysis of the end of the Middle Ages, and the history Shakespeare tells in the play is far more unhappy than comic. In the poetry of *Don Juan*, Byron indulges a digression to bemoan the loss of the Romances in *Don Quixote*'s laughter: *Cervantes smiled Spain's chivalry away; / A single laugh demolish'd the right arm / Of his own country;— seldom since that day / Has Spain had heroes*. But laughingly complain as Byron might, the simple fact is that Cervantes won, his work too good not to provide us with permanently comic lenses through which to view that lost time. And as heirs to modernity's victory, the artists of eighteenth-century England no longer had to spend much time contemplating their escape from the comic failures of the late Middle Ages. The Gothic novels of the eighteenth century, from Horace Walpole's *The Castle of Otranto* (1764) through Jane Austen's parody in *Northanger Abbey* (1818), actually emerge from a sentimental hunger *for* the supernatural thickness of lost medievalism. (As did, one could suggest, something like John Henry Newman's post-conversion 1848 novel, *Loss and Gain* and a line of British Catholic-tinged writing that would last at least through the aesthetes of the 1890s.)

Meanwhile, in the main line of the English novel—in the works of Watt's central figures of Defoe, Richardson, and Fielding—the comic and tragic possibilities of the new age proved too interesting in themselves to bother much with attacking a distant and defeated age. *Robinson Crusoe*, *Clarissa*, and *Tom Jones* are modern because they dwell in the modern present, not because they spend much time mocking their culture's premodern past. They don't need to indulge Cervantes's extended disparaging or correcting of the late medieval era.

The smoke of the eighteenth-century English battles that involved Catholicism, from the Jacobite Rising of 1745 to the Gordon Riots of 1780, can hide from us the extent to which much of middle-class Britain—which is to say, England's class of novel readers and novel writers—heaved a great sigh of relief at the Protestant settlements of William and Mary. After the Glorious Revolution in 1688, novels were free to be modern, the old medieval systems unimportant to an English Protestantism that had made its peace with—no, that was *creating* and *sustaining*—what they perceived as the modern world.

Perhaps the point could best be phrased this way: *Don Quixote* is undoubtedly the door by which we came to the modern novel. But doors do not belong entirely to the rooms we enter through them. On the other side, they are part of the rooms we leave behind. And what we enter, after *Don Quixote*, is the English novel of the eighteenth and nineteenth centuries, by which the rest of the world's novelists would be formed. The novel, in other words, as modern. And the novel as Protestant, all the way down.

CHAPTER 3 | THE RISE OF THE NOVEL

I

The history of the novel gives us any number of explicitly, deliberately, determinedly Protestant book-length stories—just as it gives us any number of extended prose fictions that promote an explicit, deliberate, and determined Catholicism. Or Marxism. Or feminism, atheism, fascism, libertarianism, and extraterrestrialism, for that matter.

And as far as those visibly Protestant works go, we can probably set aside the ones with such a loud didactic purpose that they seem thereby overwhelmed as novels—although we would have to acknowledge the hypocrisy of disdaining openly religious Protestant teaching while refusing to let didacticism disqualify other novels, from *Les Misérables*, *Middlemarch*, and *Uncle Tom's Cabin* (whose anti-slavery moral is itself almost overpowered by the book's Protestant sermons) to *Lady Chatterly's Lover*, *The Grapes of Wrath*, and *Catch-22* (its anti-war message once mocked by the poet Philip Larkin as "the American hymn to cowardice").

We can recognize, in other words, a set of moralizing Protestant books that seem to contain little in their plotting, prose, or psychological observations to recommend them beyond their edifying purpose. Charles M. Sheldon's Christian fable *In His Steps: "What Would Jesus Do?"* (1896), for example: a book that sold 30 million copies in its day. In a perfect world, we would have time to read together the neglected book-length fiction published by the Religious Tract Society, discussing in detail Evelyn E. Green's *The Head of the House: A Story of Victory over Passion and Pride* (1888) and Mrs. Walton's *Little Faith; Or, The Child of the Toy Stall* (1880). But not today.

Even on a much higher literary level, authors can seem didactically Protestant when they indulge an explicit anti-Catholicism—as, for example, Charlotte Brontë does in her 1853 novel *Villette*. Brontë had gone to Belgium to study a decade earlier, paying for her schooling by tutoring students

23

in English. In *Villette*, she draws on the experience to show her English readers something of what European Catholicism looks like in all its rich, thick, and horrifying attraction. "Lucy Snowe," Brontë names her semi-autobiographical heroine, a young Englishwoman teaching on the Continent. And after Lucy may (or may not) have encountered the ghost of an unchaste nun who had been buried alive on the old convent's grounds—eventually, in a highly charged scene, finding the nun's habit in her own chaste bed—she announces, "God is not with Rome." Is it any surprise that Lucy decides against the Catholic conversion to which she had been urged by Paul Emanuel, her love interest and the figure who may (or may not) have drowned in what Brontë herself described as the "little puzzle" of the novel's strange ending?

Of course, *Villette* has in mind ends other than its heroine's decision against godless Rome. The nuanced psychology of the novel—the constricted Lucy, holding together her loves, her hates, and her sufferings—may be the high point of Brontë's art. Certainly it is what led both George Eliot and Virginia Woolf to declare *Villette*, even with its gothic elements, superior to the earlier *Jane Eyre* (1847).

But neither can we simply dismiss as a Protestant religious tract something like Charlotte Yonge's *The Heir of Redclyffe*, another novel with strong anti-Catholic elements from that same year of 1853. The feminist revolution in criticism over recent decades has had the good effect of bringing back into print neglected women writers, even when they do not much support a feminist reading of literature, and Yonge's reputation has risen as critics have newly encountered such surprisingly good work as her 1856 children's book, *The Daisy Chain*. Yonge's *The Heir of Redclyffe*, an enormous bestseller in Britain, may have been started as purely a didactic story by its serious High Church author. But along the way it manages a clever inversion of Romantic literature, with the Byronic loner recast as Christian hero—his secret virtues isolating him from the world just as surely as secret vices might have. In a remark (admittedly off-hand) about the dreadful books that passed for "worthy" popular fiction at the time, Henry James confessed, "Occasionally, like *The Heir of Redclyffe*, they almost legitimate themselves by the force of genius."

Even without much mention of rejected Catholicism, a resolutely Protestant setting can convey a didactic tone. It's true that such settings have been used to attack Protestant sects. You can find it in Dickens's steady mockery of the evangelical chapels, signaled even in his first fiction, *The Pickwick Papers* (1837), with the comic Reverend Stiggins. You can find it, for that matter, in books from James Hogg's *Confessions of a Justified Sinner* (1842) to (the Catholic) Flannery O'Connor's *Wise Blood* (1952), both of which can be read as disturbing satires of certain forms of Protestantism.

Still, it's hard not to notice the sectarian lesson in, for example, the all-embracing Protestant atmosphere of Louisa May Alcott's *Little Women* (1869), which opens with the March girls acting out *Pilgrim's Progress* while their clergyman father is off ministering to the Union forces fighting in what Alcott understands as the Civil War's great Protestant crusade for abolition. Even *Mansfield Park* (1814) uses the assumption of an advancing Wesleyan-tinged Protestantism to resolve the moral collapse of a family made wealthy by the West Indies slave trade—and the novel, together with *Emma* (1815), marks the broadening of Jane Austen's extraordinary art to reach even the political condition of England and the nation's spiritual character.

In discussions of Protestant stories, Harold Frederic's curious 1896 work, *The Damnation of Theron Ware*, is sometimes mentioned: a book with a definite religious purpose, for all that it is shaped as a novel. As the story moves along, the faith of Frederic's Pastor Ware is gradually corrupted by his interactions with a Catholic, an atheist, and a sexually attractive girl (who represents what Kierkegaard would have called the aesthetic life). In the end, though, he is rescued by the appropriately named Soulsbys, down-to-earth Methodist activists who sober him up and set his feet back on the ground.

Even after the flood of religious-doubt fiction in the 1880s—*The Autobiography of Mark Rutherford*, Walter Pater's *Marius the Epicurean*, Mrs. Humphry Ward's bestselling *Robert Elsmere*—the novel of "loss (with possible regaining) of faith" continued to be a well-defined category of Victorian and post-Victorian literature. For that matter, attacks on the failures and hypocrisies of Christian clergy remain an artistic pastime down to the present day. And thus it's possible to read *The Damnation of Theron Ware* in the religious-doubt line of Samuel Butler's *The Way of All Flesh* (published in 1903 but finished twenty years earlier, in the era of religious-doubt novels) or even in the hypocritical-preacher line of Sinclair Lewis's *Elmer*

Gantry (1927). Reading *The Damnation of Theron Ware* in either of those lines would make more complex the message of the author's realistic prose. Nevertheless, Frederic's eccentric book is not quite what we would want for an archetypal Protestant novel—which is why, perhaps, it remains less read even than the other titles that appear with it on lists of neglected American classics.

So, let's think a little about mainline, mainstream works, undeniable instances of the art form. John Updike's novels, for example. From the pastor Fritz Kruppenbach in *Rabbit, Run* (1960) through the theologian Roger Lambert in *Roger's Version* (1986) and the preacher Clarence Wilmot in *In the Beauty of the Lilies* (1996)—to say nothing of the philandering Reverend Tom Marshfield in *A Month of Sundays* (1975), a book thick with references to Nathaniel Hawthorne and *The Scarlet Letter*—Updike often gives prominent place to Protestant religious figures. Are his novels therefore particularly Protestant? "If there was ever such a species as the Protestant novelist," the self-described "Catholic agnostic" novelist David Lodge wrote in 1986, "Mr. Updike may be its last surviving example."

And what about that ur-American novel itself, Hawthorne's *The Scarlet Letter* (1850), far more the foundation of a literature of national self-understanding, I am convinced, than the often-cited *Moby-Dick* (1851) or *Huckleberry Finn* (1884)? Do we see *The Scarlet Letter* as a particularly Protestant book, with its setting among Boston's seventeenth-century Puritans and its figure of the Reverend Arthur Dimmesdale? Or see *The Warden* (1855) that way, the book about Anglican clergy with which Trollope began his Barsetshire chronicles? Or the letters of the fictional Reverend John Ames, with which Marilynne Robinson constructed *Gilead* (2004)?

For all of them, the answer is obviously yes—and yet, no. These books are Protestant in the sense that they contain explicitly Protestant settings. Protestant, for that matter, in the sense that they were written by practicing Protestants. And Protestant in the sense that they show the psychological, social, and metaphysical effects of Protestant theology.

Setting alone, however, is not enough to define a novel, or we would be forced to count Pasternak's *Doctor Zhivago* (1957), Grossman's *Life and Fate* (1959), and Solzhenitsyn's *One Day in the Life of Ivan Denisovich* (1962) as communist novels simply because of their setting in the Soviet Union. Similarly, the religion of the author does not necessarily determine the book, else innumerable works written in the days of the Protestant estab-lishment in Britain and the United States—everything from the 1726 *Gul-liver's Travels* to the 1960 *To Kill a Mockingbird*—would automatically be defined as Protestant simply because their authors were practicing Protes-tants of one degree or another, even though the books offer little explicitly Protestant content and often only cold comfort for Protestant readers. Fi-nally, if we are to take as the defining feature an investigation of the modern world that Protestant ideas helped create, then nearly all novels, the central stream of the art form, would be Protestant—which makes Protestantism the genus of the novel itself, rather than something identifying a particular species of novels.

II

But that point, Protestantism as the genus of the modern novel, is where we have been heading all along. In *The Rise of the Novel*, Ian Watt claims Fanny Burney as an important figure in the history of the art form, reaching with her 1778 satirical novel *Evelina* toward what Jane Austen would per-fect: a joining of two streams of the early British novel. While Samuel Richardson showed us the first stream, with the "minute presentation of daily life," Henry Fielding gave us the second, with a "detached attitude" in the narrative voice, allowing the narrator to tell the story from "a comic and objective point of view." Burney's insight and Austen's genius, in Watt's interpretation, lie in their finding a way to combine the two.

Noting what Watt would call the narrative voice of "some august and impersonal spirit of social and psychological understanding," C.S. Lewis and many others have claimed for Jane Austen the tone of Samuel Johnson, in the calm and classical modes of both Johnson's irony and Johnson's as-sured morality. But Austen is not a moralizer, however morally assured she is. G.K. Chesterton once joked that Charles Dickens had for his characters the fondness with which a father looks at his children, while H.G. Wells had for his characters the fondness with which a butcher looks at a pig. There's something to that, a nice way to divide all authors. And while Jane Austen is clearly fond of her strong-willed heroines, she does have more than a little of the butcher's eye, which she learned not from Samuel John-son but from Henry Fielding.

Nonetheless, as Harold Bloom intelligently observes, Austen descends in a far more direct line from Richardson's *Clarissa* (1748) than she descends from Fielding's *Tom Jones* (1749), just as she is in turn the direct ancestor of George Eliot and Henry James, rather than of Thackeray and Dickens. "Doubtless, Austen's religious ideas were as profound as Samuel Richardson's were shallow," Bloom notes, but *Emma* and *Clarissa* are alike in being deeply "Protestant novels without being in any way religious."

Not that the other early line of the English novel, the one that flows from Fielding, is un- or anti-Protestant. The Thackeray revealed in his letters seems an ambiguous believer. But he was delighted when he came up with a *Pilgrim's Progress* title for *Vanity Fair* (1848), and rightly so. The reference to John Bunyan's spiritual classic helped him shape the novel away from being the kind of digression-filled picaresque he always loved and toward being a leading early example of the Victorian unified art. Charlotte Brontë would dedicate *Jane Eyre* to him during the magazine serialization of *Vanity Fair*, discerning even in the unfinished story a complete and coherent satire that assumes the truth of Christian virtues in order to expose the hypocrisy of a British Christian society that fails to practice what it mouths in such pious tones.

One of the best ways to see the Protestant definition of the Victorian novel—one of the best ways to see the Victorian novel however one wants to define it—is to abandon the Edwardians' adolescent sneer that their Victorian parents and grandparents were the most hypocritical people who ever lived. Not only is the Western understanding of the vice of hypocrisy shaped by its biblical expression, but the actual writings of the Victorians demonstrate the opposite of what the Edwardians supposed and inscribed in us, their descendants, as the proper scornful picture of those Victorians.

In truth, never was there a people more obsessed with identifying and rooting out hypocrisy in all its ever-more minute forms. They wrote about it so much because it bothered them so much. The early *Oliver Twist* (1838), Dickens's second novel, is not as highly regarded by critics as Dickens's later work, but toward the end it contains a scene of unexpectedly acute psychological observation as Bill Sikes attempts to lose himself, to forget the guilt of his killing of Nancy, in heroically fighting a house fire. It's an authorial courtesy to a character that suggests Dickens was willing to treat even a murderer with sympathy—a courtesy he refused to pay the hypocrites who ran the poorhouse. The sin of hypocrisy burns like Satan's signal-fire for the Victorian novelists. Not for them the saturnine sophistication of the Continental aphorists or the Catholic cultures' droll shrug at insincerity and pretense, the comedy of the Goliard poets and Rabelais derived ultimately from the *ex opere operato* principle of sacramental theology.

In other words, the Victorians wanted a clean world, an honest world, and their novelistic social concern aims at little else. Of course, in rejecting hypocrisy, one can either denounce the behavior or reject the ideal that the behavior fails to match. The Edwardians and post-Edwardians often used the fact of hypocrisy as an argument for abolishing the entire ideal frame of the culture. But the robust line of Victorian writers, the heirs of Fielding, typically used their obsession with hypocrisy to demand reformation of the behavior.

Observing such figures as the always-moral Cheeryble Brothers in *Nicholas Nickleby* and the moral-after-being-visited-by-ghosts Scrooge in *A Christmas Carol*, both George Orwell and the French critic Louis Cazamian (thanked by Ian Watt in the preface to *The Rise of the Novel*) object that, in documenting personal evil, Dickens closed his eyes to the structural problems of social evil. The benighted novelist seemed to demand only the improbable conversion of individuals—a *philosophie de Noël*, as Cazamian scoffed.

Part of that mid-twentieth-century complaint derives simply from its era, a time in which much experience of art was forced into the categories of socialist dogma, and Victorian work like Dickens's had to be read as mostly failed novelizations of Engels's *The Condition of the Working Class in England in 1844*. But in fact, in his focus on the individual rather than the complete economic restructuring of the modern world, Dickens was very much instantiating a Protestant insight into morality, derived from a Protestant metaphysics.

However powerfully our society controls us, it is an epiphenomenon created by the metaphysical drama of the soul. However completely our culture shapes us, it remains, on the cosmic scale, only the prismatic spray tossed up by individuals acting out their individual salvation plays. Where, except in the reformation of many separate selves, could we find a solid basis for change in their society and culture? The nation remains important, particularly in its role as educator: "This boy is Ignorance. This girl is

Want," the second ghost tells Scrooge. "Beware them both, and all of their degree, but most of all beware this boy, for on his brow I see that written which is Doom." But the nation is not the actual object of grace and salvation. Only the individual soul has true metaphysical weight and consequence, and the novel is the story of a soul's journey.

III

If the individual soul's journey increasingly defines the social line of the English novel from Fielding through the eighteenth-century picaresques of Smollett and on to Thackeray and Dickens—together with writers as diverse as Mrs. Gaskell, Mark Twain, and James Joyce; novels as different as *Moby-Dick*, *Crime and Punishment*, and *Herzog*—so even more does it define the personal line that runs from Richardson through Jane Austen and Henry James and down to Alice Walker and innumerable others.

I confess there's something in this kind of novel I find tedious. Austen and James, many others in the Richardson line, are beyond carping; to prefer Dickens to them is as individually revealing and critically pointless as preferring the planet Mercury to the planet Mars. Still, I do prefer *Wuthering Heights* to *Jane Eyre*, *War and Peace* to *Madame Bovary*, *Death Comes for the Archbishop* to *The Awakening* (and Rabelais to them all). Reading *The Yellow Wallpaper*, or *The Story of an African Farm*, or even much of Virginia Woolf, I find myself tiring of the relentless search inside the psyche, the endless dwelling on internal reality, as though feelings and thoughts about the self were as important and interesting as actions and thoughts about the external universe.

Except that feelings and thoughts about the self actually *are* important. They were important even in the premodern Aristotelian and Stoic rational accounts of the good life, although they were understood mostly as tools: instruments to be left behind once virtue had been achieved. And feelings and internal consciousness become more than important—they become vital—in the modern turn to the self.

This is what the novel as an art form emerged to address, and what the novel as an art form encouraged into ever-greater growth. The inner life, self-consciousness as self-understanding, becomes the manifestation of virtue and the path for grasping salvation. It's there in 1813 when Jane

Austen has Elizabeth Bennett declare, "Till this moment I never knew myself," in the great turning point of *Pride and Prejudice*, and it's there in 1908 when E.M. Forster has Lucy Honeychurch exclaim that she has at last seen for herself "the whole of everything at once," in the great turning point of *A Room with a View*—Forster's most Austen-like book, intended (as he described it in his diary) to be "clear, bright, and well constructed."

Plenty of novels, and perhaps the majority of stories told outside the novel tradition, lack thick characters with revealed interior lives. In much of the genre fiction of our time—science fiction, mysteries, and thrillers; romances, westerns, and Napoleonic War sea-stories, for that matter—the thinness of the characters can be a benefit, keeping clear the fact that those characters are acting in a kind of *chanson de geste*. They instantiate recognizable types, and they perform iconic actions. In the *roman* tradition (which is to say, in the central stream of the modern novel), the characters are generally required to be fuller: to have unique and individual interior lives. They are required to be *realistic*, the novelists say, although the range of novelistic interior lives contains its own share of well-defined types.

More to the point, such books seek to explain (and by explaining, validate and make ever more central) the kind of distinct and self-conscious self whose invention in modernity is suggested by its absence in previous literature. This is why we hesitate, backing and filling a little, when asked to name as novels such ironic eighteenth-century *chanson* fiction as Voltaire's *Candide* and Samuel Johnson's *Rasselas*, but do not hesitate at all to give the name to Sarah Fielding's minor book of *roman* fiction, *The Countess of Dellwyn*—although all three were published in the same year, 1759, forty years after *Robinson Crusoe* and a hundred and fifty years after *Don Quixote*.

The self-investigation of the self, the attempt to discern the truth amidst the clash of feelings with perceptions of social and physical reality, emerges as the proper spiritual journey of individuals and the true rightwising of their souls: *Pilgrim's Progress*, rewritten in self-consciousness. This is the purest stream of the modern novel, however much we like Dickens—however much we understand the outward peregrinations of Nicholas Nickleby, David Copperfield, and Pip Pirrip as reflecting an inward journey toward mature self-understanding. And this stream has its wellspring in Clarissa Harlowe.

When Samuel Richardson began publishing *Clarissa* in 1748, he was determined to compose a story that responded to the charges of licentious-ness against his 1740 novel *Pamela* (and to Fielding's mockery in his 1741 parody *Shamela*). *Pamela* caries the subtitle *Virtue Rewarded*, and it unsur-prisingly ends with the heroine's successful marriage as she reforms her former jailer and converts him into a true husband. And yet, *Clarissa* is the more triumphant book, even though it culminates in its heroine's death. Clarissa Harlowe's virtues are the stronger for their *not* being rewarded, the more edifying for belonging to her alone.

We tend to remember only Clarissa's long struggle to keep her integrity despite the selfish machinations of her family, and her long struggle to keep her chastity while held prisoner by a man willing to use even drugs and rape to bring her body, her mind, and her will into his possession. But Richardson devotes most of the final third of the enormously long episto-lary book to Clarissa *after* her final escape from Lovelace, and 300,000 words given over to her damaged health and consequent death. And why not? It's here that Clarissa reaches her clearest expressions of her strength and her will to be true to her ideal self.

The heroine of *Pamela* wants to keep her sexual integrity, yes, but she also wants to change others and modify the world to match her own virtue, returning to marry the contrite Mr. B in the second half of the book. The heroine of *Clarissa* is a far more passive character, externally, just as she is a far more active character, internally—which makes her the original behind Jane Austen's Fanny Price, Charlotte Brontë's Lucy Snowe, and Virginia Woolf's Mrs. Dalloway (whose first name is also Clarissa). Richardson's Clarissa Harlowe demands no real change of heart in anyone else, and she seeks to modify the world only insofar as she needs that world to leave her alone.

Of course, the consequence is that she would burn to the ground every-thing around her, if that's what it takes to be left to herself—and she nearly does. No one who tries to manipulate or use her escapes the encounter with Clarissa unscathed. But that is as must be. The "divine Clarissa" has serious internal business to do: the willing of herself into self-integrity, a matching of her self-understanding and self-possession to the virtuous pattern of the salvation to which she has been elected. For most of the novel, she either does not understand or does not care that her beauty is itself a force in the world, sexually active in ways she does not wish to be. In the long time of her dying, however—as the conversion of the rake John Belford into her defender proves—Clarissa's pale beauty is clarified beyond sexual attractiveness into a pure expression of her sanctification. No wonder Lovelace, shot in a duel with another of Clarissa's defenders, dies with the prayer "let this expiate" on his lips.

I don't know what more a reader could want for a Protestant art form. And there *Clarissa* sits, a million words near the beginning of the literature: the defining wellspring, the inescapable origin, of one of the few streams down which the entire modern project of the novel will run.

IV

It's curious that while we can speak, at least in a loose way, of the Richardson line and the Fielding line in the English novel, it is almost impossible to draw from Daniel Defoe's *Robinson Crusoe* any direct influence on the serious works of the art form. But still, somehow, everyone agrees that the novel occupies an enormous place in the foundation of the new literature.

One set of books, commonly called "Robinsonades," obviously does owe its existence to *Robinson Crusoe*. Often appearing as children's books, the genre runs from *The Female American* (1767) through *The Swiss Family Robinson* (1812) to—oh, I don't know, R.M. Ballantyne's *The Coral Island* (1857), I suppose, or Jules Verne's *Castaways of the Flag* (1900), or Andy Weir's surprise bestseller, *The Martian* (2014), or wherever one arbitrarily stops counting. But these books typically manage to be descendants of Defoe only in the broad sense of imitating the deserted-island setting and the plot of systematic organization of the means of survival, using modern knowledge in a primitive place. *The Swiss Family Robinson*, for example, is Protestant work of an obvious kind, in that it was written by a Swiss pastor and contains regular notice that the shipwrecked family is pious and often prays. But only incidentally does the story contain the Protestant view of the self that *Robinson Crusoe* gave the genre of the novel, and never does it reach toward the deeper interior journey with which Defoe infused his own work. Not even the Robinsonades, the self-declared imitators, follow the moral aim, the long-winded and imprecise prose style, or even the awkward narrative structure that Defoe gave his novel. In many ways, *Robinson Crusoe* is an isolated oddity in the history of the English novel.

And yet, it is also by universal critical agreement, one of the most consequential English novels ever written. Perhaps we can resolve the contradiction by suggesting that the 1719 *Robinson Crusoe* comes to us as something like the ground on which *Clarissa* could begin to flow in 1748 and *Tom Jones* in 1749—that is, not a stream itself, but the necessary condition for the possibility of those streams. And the ground is established in the novel's earliest moments, when Crusoe admits, "I was to be the willful Agent of all my own Miseries," rejecting his father's advice to enter business and going instead to sea in what he calls his "Original Sin."

If *Clarissa* is a tale of sanctification, then *Robinson Crusoe* is the necessary prior story: a tale of salvation and awareness of being born again. The isolated hero learns to see as "the Work of Providence" all that has happened to him—and thereby becomes master of the island on which he is stranded. Nearly dying of fever in the summer of 1660, he offers "the first Prayer, if I may call it so, that I had made for many Years." And as he recovers, we reach the central moment of the novel. Robinson Crusoe finally reads the Bible he has brought from the wrecked ship, and—without a church community or a teacher to aid him, sheerly from the power of the divine text itself on an individual conscience—he writes, "I threw down the Book, and with my Heart as well as my Hands lifted up to Heaven, in a kind of Extasy of Joy, I cry'd out aloud, *Jesus, thou Son of David, Jesus, thou exalted Prince and Saviour, give me Repentance!*" (It would be interesting, if beyond our scope here, to think about Protestant art's use of the religious memories of childhood, that old-time religion, to provide what Catholics would understand as the interpretive guides of ecclesial tradition and the deposit of faith.)

As the critic Philip Zaleski observes, it was once common to read *Robinson Crusoe* this way—to take the novel as it takes itself, a Presbyterian tale of justification and redemption revealed to its hero by adversity in God's great plan and care for the individual sinner. Perhaps Defoe's religious sense suggested writing a story of isolation, or perhaps the author merely began a story of isolation (inspired by the nonfiction 1712 accounts of Alexander Selkirk's adventures) and found thereby a way to express his religious sense. Regardless, he created with Crusoe's island something like the ideal of novelistic setting for a tale of a Protestant worldview: The journey of the self is the deepest, truest thing in the universe, and the individual soul's salvation is the great metaphysical drama played out on the world's stage. Could Clarissa Harlow have been as isolated in herself, if Robinson Crusoe had not first been shipwrecked alone on his island?

Unfortunately, Karl Marx, not otherwise known for his literary criticism, used *Robinson Crusoe* as a model text of modern capitalism in his 1867 *Das Kapital*—writing, "Of his prayers and the like we take no account." And thereby Marx established a new standard way to read the novel. *Robinson Crusoe*, we were all to understand, was an account of the economics of modernity's rising middle class and its effect on the West's imperial expansion.

The genius and impishness of Max Weber's 1905 *The Protestant Ethic and the Spirit of Capitalism* was that it turned Marx on his head. The economic condition of the rising middle class didn't create Protestantism, the book argued; Protestantism created the conditions necessary for capitalism, and culture is driven, even in its economic forms, by religion and spiritual anxieties. But Weber's work did not provide a rescue for *Robinson Crusoe*. By the time we reach R.H. Tawney's much more British-centered 1926 *Religion and the Rise of Capitalism*, Defoe's novel has become completely intertwined with economic questions—until (as the critic Irvin Ehrenpreis has pointed out) in mid-century the influential New Marxist critic György Lukács could systematically analyze the history of the novel as reflecting the history of bourgeois consciousness, with Defoe's central role "casually taken for granted."

Crusoe's island and his treatment of the native Friday were taken as unconscious metaphors for European colonizing, with imperialism understood as "the highest stage of capitalism" (to use Lenin's 1917 phrase). We shouldn't downplay Defoe's monetary fascinations; surpassing even Jane Austen and Anthony Trollope, the man is rivaled only by Benjamin Franklin and perhaps James Joyce in *Ulysses*. From *Robinson Crusoe* to *Roxanna*, Defoe was always convinced that he was revealing something important about his characters by recounting down to the farthing how much money they have in their pockets. But that kind of bookkeeping is neither the center of the novel nor, really, the gift it gave the subsequent history of the art form. It is, in a sense, only the dross of a setting at a particular time, like the rest of the social, political, and cultural facts circumstantially known to the author because he happens to be writing in a certain era.

What *Robinson Crusoe* provides the form of the novel comes rather from its sense of purpose. The individual figures in novels undergo travails and adventures, whether comic, bawdy, and ironic (as in Fielding's 1749 *Tom Jones*) or more tragicomically serious (as in his 1751 *Amelia*). And it all aims toward resolving an external situation by revealing its parallels with the characters' internal situation. Before *Robinson Crusoe*, we could have something like the 1715 French *Gil Blas*, the picaresque of one damn thing after another, but afterward we get the English revision that gradually remakes the European novel of action, from Goldsmith's *The Vicar of Wakefield* in 1766 to Thackeray's *The Luck of Barry Lyndon* in 1844.

With all its awkward proto-novel clunkiness, wordiness, and bulky digression, *Robinson Crusoe* has something close to the opposite of the great ambition of a unified art form at which the High Victorian novels aimed. Nonetheless, with Defoe, we arrive at the modern novel in its essence: a deeply Protestant book about the great journey, the only metaphysically true story, of the individual soul struggling with itself in this world that God, in his Providence, has made.

V

In a 2015 pamphlet about Catholicism and the arts, the poet Dana Gioia wrote, "Catholic literature is rarely pious. In ways that sometimes trouble or puzzle both Protestant and secular readers, Catholic writing tends to be comic, rowdy, rude, and even violent."

And in a brief online reply, the Protestant theologian D.G. Hart suggested that "perhaps the problem is that Protestants are too devout and guard what qualifies as genuinely Christian while non-Protestant Christians are more used to the big tent of mixing and matching." Admitting the "the paucity of Protestant novelists"—by which he seems to mean something like the difficulty he would have assembling a Protestant parallel to Gioia's list of Catholic writers—Hart concluded with a dismissal of both Gioia and the project of identifying religious fiction: "Protestants intuitively know (but often refuse to admit) that novels don't need to be Christian, that the question of whether a novel is Christian is actually silly."

Silly is a curious word to use for either Gioia's particular study or the more general search for the truths of Christianity in a major art form of

Western Christendom for nearly three centuries—especially when the complaint is made by someone writing in English. The greatest contributions of Great Britain and the United States to the arts have come in literature, after all. We could lose the paintings of all Anglophones, just as we could lose their classical-music compositions, without absolutely terminal damage to the history of those arts. But the novel would be destroyed beyond repair.

Still, Hart is not exactly wrong. Novels don't need to seem especially Christian to Protestant readers and writers, because the novel itself is a Protestant-inflected art form—always influenced by the definitions it obtained from its birth in English literature as a central art of Western culture: the device by which, more than any other, modernity tried to understand itself.

Consider, for example, this stray bit of information. In 1862, a Catholic priest named William Henry Anderdon published a dreadful novel called *The Adventures of Owen Evans, the Catholic Crusoe.*

In truth, that judgment may be too harsh. Anderdon could actually write, and if his novel has sunk to the bottom of the sea of time, unremembered and unmourned, still it stayed afloat for a while in its day—going through a few editions and attracting notice in the Catholic press. *The Catholic Crusoe* (as the title came to be shortened) may seem short-lived dreck, when compared with the enduring works of the era. London, that same year of 1862, saw new novels by Anthony Trollope and George Eliot, with the rest of Europe contributing Turgenev's *Fathers and Sons*, Hugo's *Les Misérables*, Flaubert's *Salammbô*, and Dostoevsky's *House of the Dead*. But considered instead in the lesser genre of Victorian apologetic fiction, *The Catholic Crusoe* ranks well above many of its contemporaries. Readers can peruse this book now without their eyes rebelling against their forced labor.

Of course, by deliberately rewriting Defoe's 1719 *Robinson Crusoe*, Anderdon invites comparison with classic authors of English literature. And though *The Catholic Crusoe* loses the contest for enduring literary power, it nonetheless offers some valuable resources for thinking about the project of Catholic fiction—of Catholic work in the art-form of the novel.

We have been arguing that, down in the eighteenth-century roots, novels as an art form took the shape of a deeply Protestant literature, which has always made Catholic novel-writing a curiously convoluted task. But regardless of the general religious tone of English fiction, Anderdon (like many others) took *Robinson Crusoe* as a particularly Evangelical and Puritan work. In the nineteenth century's theological and social battles between Protestants and Catholics, *Robinson Crusoe* needed an answer precisely because it seemed so important to the art form and so completely Protestant. For Anderdon and his readers, *The Catholic Crusoe* was not just a novel. It was an argument about how the history of English fiction would be different if it had rested on a Catholic foundation.

W.H. Anderdon remains an interesting figure. Born in 1816, he came from that enormously productive intellectual class of Victorians that included his uncle, Cardinal Manning. Educated at King's College, London, and Oxford, he was ordained as an Anglican priest in 1840—but, caught up in the Oxford Movement, he resigned his vicarage and was received into the Catholic Church in 1850. Ordained in 1853, he went on to do a little administration (not entirely unsuccessfully) at John Henry Newman's Irish university, serve his famous uncle as a secretary, and teach—while pouring out fiction, sermons, apologetics, and controversial works. ("Ever busy writing," as his brief entry in the 1913 *Catholic Encyclopedia* remarks, a little snarkily.) Joining the Jesuits in 1872, he continued to teach and write until his death at the Jesuits' Manresa House in the London suburbs in 1890.

So what would *Robinson Crusoe* have looked like if it were written by this man—a reasonably good writer, a productive controversialist, and a serious Victorian Catholic, straight from the Oxford Movement? *The Catholic Crusoe* is narrated by a Welsh surgeon named Owen Evans who spends four years (instead of Crusoe's twenty-eight) on an island where he was marooned by a wicked ship captain (instead of Crusoe's shipwreck).

In such works as *Victorian Reformations* (2013), the critic Miriam Burstein has bravely undertaken the Stakhanovite task of reading the corpus of Victorian apologetic fiction, both Protestant and Catholic, and she notes that one key difference is that Crusoe is alone for much of his novel, while Evans is part of a group. More than plot variance is at stake here. It derives from—and expresses—Anderdon's Catholic sense of God's work not only in the individual but in community. And in a community that is not some random collection of lifeboat refugees, for a key figure in the group is a priest named Don Manuel. "This figurative church," as Burstein observes, "soon becomes a literal one thanks to Don Manuel's evangelism." There's a necessary sharing of goods (with Acts 4:32 referenced), and gradually, through a series of adventures and deeds more improbable than even Crusoe's, they establish a life on their island much like Crusoe's after his finding of Friday.

But where Crusoe takes charge of the island as his English colonial property (which is why Karl Marx read Defoe's book as a foundational text in the rise of imperialism), *The Catholic Crusoe* insists on the transnationalism of the community the marooned people have formed, in parallel to the transnationalism of the Catholic Church. Where Protestantism, in Anderdon's view, claims the earth's land as potential colonies and its people as potential slaves, Catholicism understands the weakness of claims to property and wants to raise the native populations to the equality all share at Mass.

Perhaps even more to the theological point is the treatment of the sanctifying effects of work and the dignity of labor. Where Catholic novels generally present work as reenacting Christ's suffering (urging the most painful, humiliating, and self-sacrificing labor), Protestant novels generally see work as something positive and more directly sanctifying.

The resulting narrative, in Anderdon's hands, is Victorian anti-Protestant controversialism of a surprisingly high order. Anderdon grasps the Puritan center of *Robinson Crusoe* and inverts into a claim of Catholic superiority. The colonial ownership of the island ends with the island's destruction in a volcanic explosion—for property is temporary, and only the conversion to Catholicism is gained by the people who lived there. Rescued at last by a Spanish ship, Evans settles back in Protestant England (where "being a Catholic stood in my way at every turn"), while Don Manuel continues his proselytizing far off on another pagan island (with narrative hints that he will be martyred).

If Anderdon is right in *The Catholic Crusoe*, then a genuinely Catholic fiction would have to insist on community, rather than the individual's state of mind, and that insistence would usually require the presence of a priest so the sacraments can perform their communal function. It would allow the direct action of the supernatural in miracles and wonders—even while, in its endings, it would tend to find the physical world an unsatisfactory, if not a downright deceptive, arena for either justification or sanctification.

It would not typically see marriage as the definitive completion of the plot-arc of fiction. It would think of labor in terms of sanctifying travail. And it would be prone in its endings to a violence that perhaps presages the Apocalypse but certainly destroys the settled conclusions toward which novels often aim.

The American historian of the Victorian age, Gertrude Himmelfarb, once suggested that if we want to understand an era, we need to study to its second-rate thinkers even more than its first-rate thinkers. And similarly, it may be that the deep problems and deep successes of the novel as an art form are more visible in mediocre work than in the classics of the genre. Fr. Anderdon's *Catholic Crusoe* isn't good enough to answer the question of Catholic fiction, but it's good enough to pose for us that question—forcing Catholics artists to ask how much of Defoe's Protestant art form is left for them, when they try to write novels as Catholics.

In the end, we arrive at a suggestion that to write a Catholic novel is to attempt something a little tricky, a little verging on the self-contradictory. And when a Catholic or Catholic-aiming novel fails, it typically fails because it is at war with its own form. So, for instance, G.K. Chesterton's small disaster, *The Man Who Was Thursday* (1908): a piece of allegorical fiction possessing many wonderful characteristics, without "being coherent as a novel" among them. John Kennedy Toole's 1980 Catholic comedy, *A Confederacy of Dunces*, is often called Rabelaisian, but the word is accurate only relative to other modern fiction. In hard truth, we cannot simply go back to Rabelais and start over, pretending the march of modernity and the parallel histories of the novel and the self hadn't happened (much as I, as a Catholic reader, wish that we could; much as it's possible to interpret several late-twentieth-century literary movements, especially magic realism, as attempts at that return).

To write a Protestant novel is, instead, to do something a little unnecessary, a little verging on the redundant. And when a deliberately Protestant novel fails, it often fails because it seems didactic and preachy, engaged it what the art form itself promises that readers can take for granted. Hesba Stretton's *Little Meg's Children* (1868) is unbearable now, however worthy the lessons of the book may be: its tale of the abuse of poor children overrun by its sermons on Evangelical religion. *Oliver Twist* does the greater Protestant work with less concern for Protestant catechetics.

Many different campgrounds and overlooks, enclaves and inns, are available for writers as they walk the paths of the novel, and Gioia is surely right that the Catholic one remains interestingly large and robust. But the land itself is Protestant territory. Modernity's sense of the self surely owes a great deal to the philosophers, from Descartes to Kant, who theorized about it. But in its near-univeral appearance in the culture, that sense of self owes more to the novel as an art form—a form created, defined, and sent on its way, everywhere in the world, by the English-language authors confidently breathing a Protestant air.

And as the atmosphere grows thinner and thinner in the West as confidence fails, where shall we seek our future arts, our future selves?

CHAPTER 4 | THE DECLINE OF THE NOVEL

I

Back in 2011, I chanced on a news report of Billy Hunter, executive director of the NBA Players Association, proudly telling sports reporters, "I don't read fiction. I only read stuff I can learn something from." And I wanted to laugh, except that I've heard similar lines too often for it to be funny anymore. "I'm a reader," a smart, accomplished political activist told me, "a true reader, and there just aren't a lot of us left." She may be right about how many readers are left, but even a little conversation revealed what she meant. She has the self-image of being a reader, because she reads a lot of new books about politics and follows a small set of mystery writers, with almost no other new fiction.

And well she ought to call herself a reader. Don't get me wrong. Plenty of first-rate nonfiction has been published in recent decades. Plenty of good fiction, for that matter, especially with genre fiction—in which our age is unrivaled even by the flickering gaslight of the late Victorians and early Edwardians who gave us iconic figures from Sherlock Holmes to Dracula. And yet, somehow, serious novels have largely disappeared from public-intellectual life. You can read them if you want, but you don't *have* to read them to participate in the serious public discourse of America. Over lunch one day, the wonderful magazine-essayist Andrew Ferguson gave me what he called the Cocktail Party Test for new books: Would you be embarrassed to show up at a get-together of writers and public-intellectual types without having read it? And the last novel he could remember for which that seemed true was Tom Wolfe's *Bonfire of the Vanities* in 1987.

When I propose the Cocktail Party Test these days, the first response I typically hear is "Who goes to cocktail parties any more?" And that response is not without its own power, as old senses of community have decayed along with the culture the community imagined itself to share.

Still, think about what the test tells us just about the novel. A fundamental art of Western civilization for hundreds of years just doesn't seem to count for much anymore. Even the hobbyists who read new fiction don't look to such books for deep explanations of the human condition. And as far as readers go, some plow their way through science fiction, westerns, thrillers, and all the rest: the green fields of genre fiction. Others spend their time with biographies of the Founding Fathers, Civil War generals, and dead presidents. Few of them seem to read new novels, and even fewer read new novels as a duty to the high art of the civilization.

A common move at this point is to blame the writers. The essayist Joseph Epstein and the late D.G. Myers are among several (often conservative) critics who have suggested that the nation's novelists have been damaged by the writing-degree aesthetic that came out of the universities' graduate schools. Oh, these critics often think, American writers were hurt by politics, too, with the mainstreaming of left-leaning thought in the academy and the sidelining of artists who failed to toe the progressive line. Economics, too, as changes in tax law helped cause the disappearance of the mid-list book in publishers' catalogues, with further damage to fiction. Where will later generations find something like John Williams's *Stoner* (1965), a novel that fell flat when first published but gradually forced its way back into notice? But really, in this line of thinking, it was the institutionalizing of writing in the dead end of the academy that taught generations of authors to use a prissy, high-gloss prose read by no one but themselves.

All this forms a nice thesis, weakened only by the fact that it seems mostly untrue. The Académie française did not eliminate novels among the nineteenth-century French, although it had a stronger influence on a national literature in the 1870s than any American academy has ever had. And leftist politics was, if anything, more important to the great writers of the 1930s than to the fading writers of the 1990s. Besides, novels are hardly the only art to decay. When was the last time America's lost novel readers cared about a new opera? Poetry failed the Cocktail Party Test somewhere around the death of W.H. Auden in 1973. Sculpture got gobbled up by its own theory long before Henry Moore died in 1986. You can be a lively and cultivated partygoer these days without being able to name a living painter, composer, or playwright you admire.

Throughout these pages, the suggestion has been that our problems with the novel are deeper than changes in college writing departments can address—for the cause is a failure of nerve not in art but in metaphysics. If novelists themselves don't believe there exists a deep structure of morality and manners that can be discerned by the novel, why should readers believe it? Why should they care? When people in other nations speak of Western culture, they typically mean nothing more than movies and pop music, and how could we tell them they are wrong? Besides Hollywood, television, and the recording industry, the Western nations in general, and the Anglophone nations in particular, have produced few major (meaning world-historical) works of art since about 1975. Maybe since 1950. The music reviewer and librettist Terry Teachout once conceived the idea of asking critics in various artistic disciplines to name the great modern works of their field—dance, symphony, sculpture, painting, poetry, novels—and hardly a single answer he received was from after the first decades of the twentieth century.

These things run in cycles, and what goes down may come up. But I was at a conference a few years ago—one of those "Seeking Literature" things that get called together from time to time—and I must have heard at least three talks demanding that we "defend culture" from the Vandals within and the Visigoths without. Lord knows, there's plenty of defending that needs to be done. But mostly I found myself thinking, *Why, exactly?* What is the culture you think we are supposed to defend?

II

We have been arguing that the novel emerged in eighteenth-century Britain both to reveal and to solve a particular problem of the modern Protestant self. And as the novel grew, increasingly becoming a dominant art form across Western culture, its success proved that the modern problem was bigger and more pervasive than just a eighteenth-century moment on a dreary set of British islands in the North Sea. It was spread across the European-defined world, from the Americas to Russia, and it was shared to a significant degree by Protestants, Catholics, the Orthodox, and atheists alike. In fact, by exposing the problem so successfully, the novel exacerbated the problem's effect. Readers learned to notice their troubled modern selves by reading novels aimed at solving the troubles.

That's not to dismiss the ongoing influence of Protestantism, for the Reformation was, to use again Max Weber's description, one of the elective affinities that helped create the modern world, even for those who were not Protestants. Discovering the old scientific phrase through Goethe's use of it as a literary metaphor, Weber deployed "elective affinities" to argue that social facts will sometimes gravitate toward one another and become interrelated, even though no direct cause impels them. His most famous (and disputed) example is the elective affinity of Protestantism and economic investment in northern Europe, but perhaps we can speak loosely of an even broader interrelation.

Scientific thinking, inventiveness, the impulse toward democracy, the rise of the nation-state, the standardizing of bureaucracy, the economic interests of the emerging middle class, the spirit of Enlightenment rationalism, and Protestantism all acted as elective affinities. However much they logically need not have joined together, they *did* join, creating a powerful social force that propelled European culture out of the Middle Ages. Neither a shopkeeper in Marseille nor a government file clerk in Moscow was likely to be Protestant in 1860. But by owning a bourgeois shop or working for a central government's bureaucracy, they had entered the modern world, and their sense of self was increasingly modern—which is to say, generally inflected by the Protestant worldview.

They also tended to be novel readers, or at least the people for whom novels were written. The magisterial novel, first as a rising and then as a dominant art form, existed in a relatively narrow period of time in the history of the world: less than three hundred years, from the publication of Daniel Defoe's *Robinson Crusoe* in 1719 to the appearance of, say, V.S. Naipaul's *A Bend in the River* in 1979. Or Martin Amis's *Money* in 1984. Or David Foster Wallace's *Infinite Jest* in 1996, or wherever one wants to pause the accounting. Not coincidentally, that was also the period of the great established Protestant hegemony in some of the most powerful nations of the West.

Our analysis of the novel has concentrated on English-language works, but that is not solely because of linguistic chauvinism and the monoglotic infirmity that has always infected English speakers. It also reflects the fact that the modern novel starts as an English-language growth, planted and cross-fertilized in the Protestant hothouses of Great Britain and the United

States. The novel in English—and in other European languages, through the influence of the extraordinary burst of English fiction in the eighteenth and nineteenth centuries—depends on what we earlier called a Protestantism of the Air, so all-surrounding that even the novel's practitioners often failed to notice it.

The legal establishment of the Anglican Church in England had been unassailable, at least among the middle class, since the coming of William and Mary in 1688, and it was increasingly a Protestant-tinged Anglicanism through the nineteenth century (despite the Catholicizing of the Oxford Movement's Keble, Newman, and Pusey). Even in America, William and Mary had an effect as the Glorious Revolution overthrew James II, a Catholic king, after the birth of a son who would guarantee a Catholic succession.

Politically, William and Mary's invasion of England in 1688 allowed the American settlers to return to the separate-colony system (the precursor to the Constitution's recognition of individual states) by abolishing the Dominion of New England, a short-lived attempt to impose a Spanish-style governor on Britain's American possessions. Culturally, however, the Glorious Revolution had something like the opposite effect, drawing the nation together. In general agreement with William and Mary's definition of Britain as essentially Protestant—essentially unified in opposition to the power of Roman Catholicism around the world—the seventeenth-century Puritans of New England began to reconcile with their fellow Protestants.

They began, in other words, to see themselves as joined to the general current of the Reformation rather than as a pilgrim people set entirely apart from the rest of believers. The result is what Tocqueville saw when he toured the United States in the early 1830s. The Protestant sects in America profoundly rejected one another theologically, and yet they somehow managed to combine socially to give the new country an "undivided current of manners and morals"—an implicit America establishment of the central stream of Reformed Protestantism.

Add in the Protestant portions of Germany, Switzerland, and France, the Lutheran fortresses of Scandinavia, the Calvinist establishment in the Netherlands, and even European Catholics could not help but breathe at least a little of the modern, Protestant-perfumed air. Certainly some Catholics would write modern novels influenced by their Catholicism; from

Balzac's *Le Père Goriot* (1834) to Huysmans's *La cathédrale* (1898), French literature alone offers work by any number of Catholic authors in the nineteenth century. But we are speaking not of individual novelists so much as the cultural establishment of the confident West. And gross and unfair as the generalization is, there's a certain rough truth to the rule that the more monolithically Catholic a European country was, the more medieval it remained, and the fewer significant novels it contributed to the corpus of nineteenth-century literature. The dominant European mood, the Protestantism of the Air, provided its novel writers with a cultural confidence: the assurance, the certainty, that the metaphysical problem of the age could be observed and possibly solved by art in general and the novel in particular.

Of course, the problem that the novel was supposed to observe and solve was what we have called the modern crisis of the self—and that too was a Protestant-tinged phenomenon. The new idea of the self was profoundly shaped by both the way the Reformation turned religious attention inward on the individual soul and the way the Reformation focused that attention by a systematic "stripping of the altars" (to borrow the title of Eamon Duffy's important 1992 study of the Protestantizing of England).

We have already discussed the fascinating newness of the modern punctual self, but that second element needs expansion—for along the way, the exterior world was gradually stripped of its supernatural meanings, even while the metaphysical weight of the interior self was growing. By rejecting the idea of natural purpose, science did its part in emptying out the world. The new economics of exchange value and the new efficiencies of bureaucracy joined in, as well. The elective affinities of modernity would prove to have at least this much in common: They all had the effect of silencing the old religious vibrations of the external world, and they all worked at erasing the medieval sense of a world filled with living symbols. Together they stripped the altars of reality. The process didn't, couldn't, happen all at once, but bit by bit, a piece here and a piece there, the West lost its sense of supernatural density. And all the weight of metaphysical significance in the world was transferred to the individual self.

Think of it in terms of the planets and stars, to use an example of C.S. Lewis's. From antiquity to the Middle Ages, it was common to see the night sky and imagine that we were *looking in*, spectators treated to view of a great intergalactic dance; "beyond the circle of the moon," as Aristotle noted, "there is no evil." In modernity we typically imagine instead that we are *looking out*—the significant center now in the viewer, examining a cold and meaningless universe.

Or think of it terms of the drama of good and evil. For the Medievals, the world was filled with saints and demons, angels and devils, ghosts, monsters, prophecies, and signs. And more often than not, human beings were pawns in, or merely spectators to, a great supernatural battle. Christ's Resurrection was *physically* true, a powerful blow struck in the cosmic war, and it echoed across the universe. In Protestant-influenced modernity, we are instead the actors, the principals, of the great drama. Christ's Resurrection is *morally* true, providing the possibility that we can discern good and evil in ourselves as we act out our lives.

For believers—which is to say, most of the Europeanized world through the nineteenth century—God Himself remained a cosmic force. But all the lower supernatural thickness of the world was reduced, packed down into the individual. What saints and demons, angels and devils, ghosts and monsters were to people in the Middle Ages, the self became to Moderns: an object of metaphysical weight in the secular world greater than anything ever contemplated before.

What we described earlier as *chanson* fiction (tales of ideal types performing symbolically charged actions, without much revealed interior self) is more than adequate, perhaps even preferable, for stories told in a world thick with supernatural realities. What we called *roman* fiction (accounts of characters with internal processes and psychological identity) becomes necessary when we wish to present human figures as something real within themselves. After modernity came to see the self as the only thick object in a thin universe, how could the novel not turn to the *roman* telling of the story of the self? Both forms of fiction derive from the same principle, the artist concerned with what seems most real. In a shifted universe, however, what seems most real is human consciousness: all supernatural reality other than God packed down into the individual soul.

No wonder a great hunger for a metaphysically thicker world, for a supernatural infusion, is written across the nineteenth and early twentieth centuries. As I note in *An Anxious Age*, my 2014 study of American religion, it's there in the séance movement that was born in Hydesville, New York—

when the Fox sisters, Kate and Margaret, reported in 1848 the rapping noises of the ghost of a murdered peddler. It's there in the crystal-ball spiritualism that enthralled innumerable liberal congregations, particularly the Hicksite branch of the Quakers, in the early days, and the Universalists, later in the century. It's there in the reasons the Aesthetes, from Oscar Wilde to Joris-Karl Huysmans, were drawn first to horror settings and then to Catholicism. It's there in the popularity of Bram Stoker's 1897 *Dracula*, for that matter.

Tarot cards, spirit photographs, magic mirrors, the American spiritualist Pearl Curran's popularizing of the Ouija board during the First World War: Western culture (meaning, especially, Protestant culture in Great Britain and the United States) was awash with claims of new ways to observe the supernatural. The fascination with clairvoyance and the occult. The rebirth of astrology. Theosophy and the revival of long-dead Eastern religions: the cult of Isis, the worship of the Thrice-Great Hermes. Their goofy flourishing in the early decades of the twentieth century suggests that Western art, even the novel, was already failing to convince the culture of re-enchantment—failing at convincing us there actually were solutions to the metaphysical crisis. The exterior world just wouldn't thicken up enough to match the thickness of the interior self.

And on and on the slow progressive failure of our belief in the novel's deepest purpose would go. Until one day—all the way back in 1987, maybe, or 2001, or 2010—even the people who understood themselves as readers had, almost unaware, turned away to genre fiction, biography, and accounts of politics. It's a sad result, but may, in hindsight, prove to have been unavoidable on the path of the modern novel as we trace it, in the following chapters, through Walter Scott's turn to history, Charles Dickens's hunt for truth, Thomas Mann's high modernist goals, and Tom Wolfe's fruitless ambitions.

CHAPTER 5 | SIR WALTER SCOTT AND THE PAST

I

By the time he published *Waverley*, his first novel, in 1814, Walter Scott already had a wide European reputation as a poet, the popular Romantic composer of poetic stories with such works as *The Lay of the Last Minstrel* in 1805 and *Marmion* in 1808. Nonetheless, he was uncertain of his skills as a writer of prose. In his 1831 autobiography, Scott claims that after showing an early version of *Waverley* to a "critical friend, whose opinion was unfavorable," he tucked the manuscript inside an old writing desk, where it remained for so long that he considered it lost. Occasionally, Scott writes, he thought of continuing his prose "romance," but was simply "too indolent to attempt to write it anew from memory." When finally Scott rediscovered the manuscript of *Waverley* (reportedly while searching the desk for the fishing tackle he thought was stored there), he set to work to complete it "according to my original purpose."

In the course of finishing *Waverley*—the first novel by the author whose popularity quickly came to dominate publishing in the pre-Victorian early years of the nineteenth century—Scott would draw on his extensive historical research and add real characters to the narrative mix. In a certain sense, *Waverley* is an early example of the *Bildungsroman*, for its central character, Edward Waverley, leaves a sheltered environment for a series of worldly encounters that carry him from romantic naiveté to a kind of maturity. (As the critic Richard Humphrey notes, "It is one of the ironies of literary history that Scott, whose work is a repeated critique of romance, should be among the authors read by Madame Bovary when Flaubert comes to criticize her reading habits. Such is the march of realism.")

Scott himself wrote that he undertook *Waverley* to do for Scotland what Maria Edgeworth had done for Ireland in such novels as *Castle Rackrent* (1800). Scott admired Edgeworth's "rich humor, pathetic tenderness, and admirable tact." Edgeworth's books had achieved much for Ireland, he thought, for they had introduced "her natives" to English-language readers in "a more favorable light then they had been placed hitherto," while arousing "sympathy for their virtues and indulgence for their foibles."

Equally, Scott hoped to chronicle a disappearing Scotland, for "no European nation" had, he believed, "over the course of fifty or so years, undergone such a dramatic change." *Waverley* takes place in 1745, just one year before British troops demolished the forces of Charles Edward Stuart, the grandson of James II, at the Battle of Culloden. This defeat ended the Jacobite claim to the British throne—and it also instigated a series of parliamentary acts aimed at the brutal diminishing of Gaelic culture. The acts extended as far as banning Highland dress, including the kilt, and they ended the real power of clan chiefs who had supported Bonnie Prince Charlie and the Stuart cause.

In the following decades, as Scott noted, the "gradual influx of wealth, and the extension of commerce" had made "the present people of Scotland a class of beings so different from their grandfathers, as the existing English are from those of Queen Elizabeth's time." The changes also resulted from the growth of coal and lime mining, and—even more significantly—from an explosion in sheep farming that, by the end of the eighteenth century, made Scotland a leading exporter of wool. As more and more sheep arrived, increasing numbers of rural Scots emigrated, particularly to Canada and the United States. The construction of new and better roads, particularly from London to Edinburgh, inevitably contributed to the further Anglicization of Scotland.

"Scotland, which had joined the United Kingdom in the Union of 1707 was now feeling the full brunt of that change—in increased commercialism, creeping Anglicization and the steady ousting of Scots as a language," as Richard Humphrey observes. "Some Scotsmen were beginning to call themselves North Britons and, as David Daiches has nicely pointed out, it was a Scotsman who wrote 'Rule Britannia!' and another who founded the *Encyclopedia Britannica* (1771). All in all, the great social historian T.C. Smout has written, the Scotland of Scott's lifetime is 'a watershed between one kind of society and another.'"

Scott did not wholly lament these changes. He was himself enormously ambitious, an investor, landowner, and author who would reap vast sums for the international success of his books. He identified with the values and attitudes of both the Scottish Enlightenment and the Tory landowning class, and his support for the Hanoverians grew so pronounced that George IV, as prince regent, invited Scott to dine in 1815. In 1822, as king, sporting a kilt, he paid a much celebrated visit to Edinburgh at Scott's behest. The writer was no foe of commercial or scientific progress, and he accepted entirely the belief that, in innumerable ways, the betterment of humanity inevitably required a measured and enlightened discarding of the past. As he notes in a postscript to *Waverley*, he certainly did not regret the passing of "much absurd political prejudice" associated with the Highland chiefs' "hopeless" attachment to the restoration of a Stuart king.

In fact, for Scott, "the destruction of the patriarchal power of the Highland chiefs" and the "total eradication of the Jacobite party" were entirely necessary for Britain's continued ascent as a preeminent, and Protestant, world power. The Scots' refusal to "intermingle with the English, or adopt their costumes," was nothing more than an irrational attachment to sentiments that could be cherished for their historical color, but otherwise deserved no viable place in the modern world. It was a lingering impediment to national unity and the continued growth of British power.

Scott revealed his own political assumptions in his *The Life of Napoleon Bonaparte, Emperor of the French* (1828), which John Stuart Mill famously shredded in a lengthy review in the *Westminster Review*. Mill describes Scott's "decided bias towards aristocratic persons and aristocratic opinions." But Scott, Mill adds, has adopted "a mode of writing as should be best calculated to win the good word and good opinion of everybody." Mill places Scott on "the liberal side of high Tory opinions," an "advocate of the aristocracy against the people," but "not altogether an illiberal or disingenuous one." Mill suggests that, "in political and social philosophy," Scott's "principles are all summed up in the orthodox one, that whatever is English is best; best, not for England only, but for every country in Christendom, or probably the world."

In other words, Scott was not a Scottish nationalist, but he did believe in preserving—even celebrating—a distinctive Scottish identity within the United Kingdom. And he regretted the passing of a distinctive Scots culture associated with "the folks of the old leaven," who have "now almost entirely vanished from the land." Scot would devote much of his wealth to assembling a massive collection of Scottish antiques, armaments, and artifacts, including the cross that Mary Stuart carried to her execution. These he displayed at Abbotsford, the sprawling and hugely expensive castle-like home he built for himself on an estate in the Scottish Borders, near Melrose, along the bank of the River Tweed.

The passing of the Highlanders also meant the dissipation of "many living examples of singular and disinterested attachment to the principles of loyalty which they received from their fathers, and of old Scottish faith, hospitality, worth, and honour." And it's here that we reach the core of the question Scott poses for the history of the novel as an art form.

It is common to say that a sense of progress rules modernity—modern times dominated by a narrative about how the dark medieval past is being overcome with the enlightened march of advancing humanity. The arrogance of that modern sense, the Marxists would say, leads inevitably to oppression of the working class at home and the Western imperialism everywhere else. And perhaps that is true. But what, then, are we to do with Walter Scott? With the rise of the historical novel? With the feeling, manifesting itself in fiction even before Victoria became queen, that something important was missing from modern experience?

II

The novel as an art form blossomed from English roots, we have claimed, as a presentation of the Protestant view of the self: the novel as a modern device for explaining that view, instantiating it, and solving its problems. And chief among those problems, we have also claimed, is *thinness*: the great emptying out of the supernatural order, the reduction of the metaphysical order to little beyond the bare Christian minimum of God above and the individual soul below. This is the modern phenomenon that Max Weber chose Schiller's word *disenchantment* to name—and it is the effect of the concatenation, the joining of the forces to create the modern age that (as we have noted) he chose Goethe's phrase *elective affinities* to describe.

One possible solution is to invest class and social manners with a kind of metaphysical weight that haunts the characters. It's there in Hardy's *Jude the Obscure* (1895), and there in Edith Wharton's *The Age of Innocence* (1920), and there in more novels than can be counted. This is the force behind Henry James's comic plaint about all of which Nathaniel Hawthorne had been deprived as an American—"denuded" of a European social order still rich enough that it could, in a novelist's vision, substitute for the kind of metaphysical density that Hawthorne had to conjure up for himself from New England's Puritan past. "No sovereign, no court, no personal loyalty, no aristocracy, no church, no clergy, no army, no diplomatic service, no country gentlemen, no palaces, no castles, nor manors, nor old country houses, nor parsonages, nor thatched cottages nor ivied ruins," James writes of poor Hawthorne, "no cathedrals, nor abbeys, nor little Norman churches; no great Universities nor public schools—no Oxford, nor Eton, nor Harrow; no literature, no novels, no museums, no pictures, no political society, no sporting class—no Epsom nor Ascot!"

Another possible solution is the introduction of actual supernatural elements. Certainly God himself and usually even his angels were too awe-inspiring and hence too close to blasphemy to place in a novel. But the conventions of eighteenth-century Gothic fiction allowed demons and malevolent ghosts to stalk the pages, and evil took on a reality that thickened the narrative world—sometimes so much so, as in Matthew Gregory Lewis's *The Monk* (1796), that the metaphysical evil seems to devour the entire physical world.

Yet another solution is the eighteenth-century elevation of sentiment: a thickening of the world with emotion. Indeed, at its best, the novel of sentiment contains a suggestion that certain elements of reality are somehow *broadcasting*. The sentiments we feel are not derived merely from us; they are demanded by the natural vistas, *objet d'art*, and tumbled ruins that are rich enough, weighty enough in metaphysical power, to provoke us to sentiment.

The huge success of *The Sorrows of Young Werther* (1774) tempts us to read this form of the novel as involving simply a self-willed capacity to feel greatly. It is this self-willing element, in the absence of any matching object of feeling, that Jane Austen mocks in *Sense and Sensibility* (1811), just as she mocks the willfulness of the Gothic emotion of horror in *Northanger Abbey* (1817). A more charitable reading of Henry Brooke's *The Fool of Quality* (1770) and Henry Mackenzie's *The Man of Feeling* (1771) might allow us a better way to understand what Goethe was actually aiming at with his journey into Romanticism with *The Sorrows of Young Werther*, the true classic of the genre.

These kinds of literary divisions are never clean and often arbitrary. Witness the ease with which, for instance, the novel of sentiment and the Gothic novel blend into each other. As the introduction to a modern reprinting notes, Maria Edgeworth's *Castle Rackrent* has been called the first regional novel, the first Anglo-Irish novel, the first multi-generation-saga novel, the first manor-house novel, and the first feminist novel—along with claiming a late place in the genre of sentimental novels and an early place in the genre of historical novels.

But here, with a mention of the historical novel, we can see many of these impulses beginning to merge and find a home: a thickening of the world by an appeal to the past. It's curious that one of the best-known Marxist works of literary criticism is an account of historical novels, written by a Hungarian more or less hiding out in Moscow in the 1930s. But there is no escaping György Lukács's *The Historical Novel* when one wants to think about the genre. And however much the form was invented or anticipated by works such as Sophia Lee's *The Recess* (1783), an underrated novel about the heirs of Mary Queen of Scots, Lukács is right to focus on Walter Scott, the author who taught Europe how to write this kind of story.

Through his reading of Scott, Lukács identifies what he declares characteristic features of the historical novel. The story is usually epic in its historical setting, but its fictional heroes and heroines are typically ordinary people, swept back and forth by the changing tides of the dramatic era, with real figures of historical importance making cameo appearances along the way. As the sympathetic critic Perry Anderson notes, Lukács sees Scott's novels as staging "a tragic contest between declining and ascending forms of social life, in a vision of the past that honors the losers but upholds the historical necessity of the winners. The classic historical novel, inaugurated by *Waverley*, is an affirmation of human progress, in and through the conflicts that divide societies and the individuals within them." And with this social reading of Scott, Lukács observes a deliberate technique of realism somehow dominating the Romanticism of the historical novel, and thereby he traces a direct line from *Waverley* to Tolstoy's Napoleonic setting for *War and Peace* (1869), via Balzac's post-Napoleonic setting for *La Comédie humaine* (1799–1850).

All this is possible, I suppose. But how then are we to understand what, say, Flaubert clearly thought the historical novel was, when he unexpectedly published *Salammbô* in 1862? A sensual tale set in the exotic local of Carthage in the third century B.C., the book is a deliberate putting aside of what Flaubert had achieved in 1856 with *Madame Bovary*, perhaps the most brilliantly careful realistic account of a modern psyche ever composed. Perry Anderson points out that Walter Scott had a rationalistic streak, influenced by Adam Ferguson and other figures of the Scottish Enlightenment, just as Tolstoy was taught by Stendhal and others to give a hard rationalist edge to his investigations of character, even against the nationalistic melodrama that is the background of *War and Peace*. Nonetheless, as the later Marxist Fredric Jameson suggests in his amendment of Lukács, it is no accident that Walter Scott had a great vogue among the writers of opera—for the likes of Rossini, Bellini, and Donizetti are extracting from him a purified essence of the modern telling of a historical story.

In that purer line, I would suggest, the great Russian historical novel is not Tolstoy's 1869 *War and Peace* but Nikolai Gogol's 1842 *Taras Bulba*. And in its purity, it offers a clear picture of the hunger for a metaphysically thick world that Europe was finding expressed by Walter Scott.

III

So let's think about Gogol's *Taras Bulba* for a moment. Take the wild history of the Cossacks in the Ukraine. Add the birth of nationalism and the drawing in of the principalities around Moscow to form a modern country. Include Eastern Orthodoxy's long struggle against the Catholic Poles and the Ottoman Muslims. Don't forget a love story in which a son betrays his father and his people for the sake of a beautiful daughter of the enemy. Mix in a big dollop of anti-Semitism and alternating moments of unselfconscious joy in the midst of battle and unselfconscious moroseness at night around the campfire. Finally, douse the whole thing in huge buckets of vodka, and the result can have only one name: Russia.

It's a curious thing, but perhaps the most definitive historical novel ever written appeared in a literature that hardly existed at the moment of the book's composition. In the early nineteenth century, Russia had only the thinnest gloss of modern European civilization, and, apart from the efforts of Pushkin, the Russian language had hardly produced a book that the rest of the world thought worth reading. And then came Nikolai Gogol, who, before his death in 1852 at the age of forty-three, suggested, in the barest handful of works, every path down which Russian literature would subsequently head.

An "epic poem," he called *Taras Bulba* when he transformed an 1835 short story into a novel in 1842, though the book is entirely in prose and runs only 150 pages. Nonetheless, Gogol was right. *Taras Bulba* is an epic, and it's structured like a poem. Tolstoy could not have written *War and Peace* without the epic feeling Gogol gave Russian literature—any more than Solzhenitsyn could have written *One Day in the Life of Ivan Denisovich* without the imagistic logic of poetry, rather than the narrative logic of fiction, with which Gogol endowed his nation's prose.

Taras Bulba is set in the sixteenth century, after the retreat of the Lithuanians had left the Ukraine under the intermittent rule of Poland. As the Poles struggled to absorb "Little Russia," the Ukrainians formed the military culture of the Cossacks—essentially a cross between crusaders and thieves, the center of the multi-sided fight against Poles, Turks, and Crimean Tatars. Taras Bulba himself is an aging "colonel" of the Zaporozhian Cossacks, a lifelong warrior whose two sons, Andri and Ostap, have finished their schooling at an Orthodox seminary and returned to begin their careers as mounted soldiers. Actually, the word *soldiers* conveys too much, or too little, in this context. The Cossacks, as the novel shows them, were not an organized military, but a horde; not an army, but an entire people of war—and old Taras will live to kill one of his sons for joining the enemy and watch the other son tortured to death. No wonder the boys' mother weeps as they leave at the end of the first chapter to join the Cossack camp.

Indeed, that scene of the mother's certainty that she will not see her sons again encapsulates all the peculiar compellingness of *Taras Bulba*. Here it is in Peter Constantine's translation: "As they rode out of the gate she came rushing out with the lightness of a wild goat, unimaginable at her age, held one of the horses with incomprehensible strength, and embraced her son with blind, crazed fervor. She was carried again into the house. The young Cossacks rode off sadly, holding back their tears out of respect for their father, who was perturbed himself, although he struggled not to show it. It was a gray day. The green steppes glittered brightly. Birds chattered discordantly."

What are we to do with prose like this? It lacks the logic of a novel's narrative. It is, instead a prose version of the succession of images by which an epic poem tells a story.

Even the romantic elements in *Taras Bulba* are somehow naive—as Gogol imagines Homer is naive, a naiveté achieved only at the farthest end of artfulness. When Andri, in love with a beautiful Polish girl, forsakes his family to fight beside the Poles against the Cossacks, his father shouts out to him during the battle, "These are your own people"—and Gogol adds, "But Andri could no longer tell what men were in front of him, whether they were his own people or not. He could see nothing but locks of hair, long beautiful locks, and a swan-white breast and a snow-white neck, and beautiful shoulders, all made for rapturous kisses. 'Men! Quick! Draw him over to the forest!' Taras shouted, and thirty of the swiftest Cossack riders set out to draw Andri into the forest."

Critics make much, and rightly, of Gogol's birth in the Ukraine and his use of backward, rural Ukrainian settings in his collections of stories known as *Evenings on a Farm*, which provided for Russian readers (as stories set in the South would later provide for American readers) both broad comedy and a nostalgic feeling for a world that was already passing away. Even the translated titles of those stories that made the young author's reputation—like "St. John's Eve" and "How Ivan Ivanovich Quarreled with Ivan Nikiforovich"—convey what the urban Russians found comic and sweet in them.

But it is worth remembering that by the time he wrote *Evenings on a Farm*, Gogol was already well established at the worldly solons of St. Petersburg as the protégé of Pushkin. There exists an extraordinary letter from Gogol to his mother at the time, demanding from her accounts of all the folk stories she can remember, together with all the Ukrainian details he himself never really experienced. "That is very, very necessary for me. I expect from you in your next letter a complete description of the costume of a village deacon, from his underclothes to his boots, with the names used by the most rooted, ancient, undeveloped Little Russians."

In the heartbreakingly brief literary career that followed before his death at age forty-two in 1852, it was as though Gogol set one perfect marker on each of the paths down which subsequent Russian writers would have no choice but to go. A suggestion from Pushkin produced from Gogol the comedy *The Inspector General*, from which Russian theater still has not recovered. The picaresque novel *Dead Souls* set the conditions all later comic fiction would have to obey. And then there are the short stories—so few, and yet each pregnant with what would become the history of Russian literature: "Nevsky Prospect," "Viy," "The Diary of a Madman." Dostoyevsky brought something very Russian to completion with *Notes from Underground*, but Gogol had pointed the way with "The Overcoat." The absurd that runs through Russian literature was simultaneously born and transcended in his story "The Nose."

Along the way, Gogol set himself to study his nation's history—even teaching it (briefly and badly, by all reports) at the university in St. Petersburg. His letters about his studies swing back and forth. At some moments, he gladly folds the history of Little Russia into the emerging history of the Greater Russian behemoth. At other moments, he sees the Muscovites and White Russians as the great betrayers of Ukrainian culture.

Though he intended to write a multi-volume nonfiction history, his obsessive historical research issued instead only in the 150 pages of *Taras Bulba*. Both his distaste for White Russia and his Greater Russian nationalism are discernable in the book, which makes the book difficult to place in the usual categories of historical fiction. But he wanted, from his tiny epic poem in prose, more than just a chance to play in the fields of history. He aimed somehow both to celebrate the platonic ideal of Russia and to escape from all the modern reality that Russia was becoming. That, too, is very Russian: yet another theme from which his successors could not break free. Gogol wanted to find the unmodern mind and dwell within it for himself.

Make no mistake. The Cossacks of *Taras Bulba* are monsters, by any modern standard. If a battle goes well, they drink themselves into madness and skewer a few Polish babies to celebrate. It a battle goes poorly, they drink themselves into madness and drown some Jews to assuage their grief. But, like all real monsters in the age of mythology, they have an innocence as well—the violent innocence of unself-consciousness, the brutal innocence of Homer's warriors. "Good, my son, good!" Taras weeps, watching and unable to help as his son Ostap refuses to cry out while the Poles torture him to death. "You did well by those Poles, didn't you?" he proudly asks his other son Andri before he shoots him for his treason.

To the world of "The Diary of a Madman," "The Overcoat," and "The Nose"—the comic and wrenching world of the modern urban Russia he saw before him, with all its hyper-selfconsciousness, resentment, hypocrisy, weakening Orthodox faith, and unrootedness—*Taras Bulba* is Gogol's answer. The reader who cannot feel the horror of that answer has not absorbed the ethical turns of modernity, set in place by the Protestant origins of the novel. But the modern reader who cannot understand why there is a lure in that answer has not understood the modern problems of thinness that caused the genre of the historical novel to appear.

IV

Waverley starts sluggishly. It is not surprising that a friend advised him to toss it away, or that Francis Jeffrey in the *Edinburgh Review* described its opening chapters as "laborious" and "considerably below mediocrity." Scott was finding his way in an unaccustomed format: a novel built on a platform of historical fact.

In Chapter 3, however, he offers a detailed and amusing psychological profile of the novel's central character, Edward Waverley, who will leave a sheltered modern world for a far wilder one, where he will eventually find himself and, after much turmoil, manage to tame his "wavering and unsettled habit of mind." Young Waverley, we learn, was largely neglected by his father, a prosperous merchant with close links to the Whig party and the House of Hanover. Edward is essentially reared by his uncle, Sir Everhard Waverley, who presides over Waverley-Honour, a vast estate in Hampshire. Sir Everhard is a Tory whose nostalgic admiration of to the Stuarts is passed along to Edward.

In the story, Sir Everhard sets out to educate his nephew and provides him with a tutor. Of course, Everhard "had never been himself a student" and held the view that "the mere tracing of the alphabetical characters with the eye is in itself a useful and meritorious task, without considering what ideas or doctrines they may happen to convey." Edward's tutor, moreover, is distracted and indulgent, and so Edward roams at will in "the library at Waverley-Honour, a large Gothic room, with double arches and a gallery," which "contained such a miscellaneous and extensive collection of volumes as had been assembled together, during the course of two hundred years, by a family which had been always wealthy, and inclined, of course, as a mark of splendour, to furnish their shelves with the current literature of the day, without much scrutiny or nicety of discrimination." Young Waverley "drove through the sea of books like a vessel without a pilot or a rudder." And, not surprisingly, Edward (like the young Walter Scott, who contracted polio as a child and spent much of his boyhood sunk in books) is drawn particularly to Spenser, Drayton, and "other poets who have exercised themselves on romantic fiction." He devours numerous imitations of the *Decameron* and the romances of Froissart, "with his heart-stirring and eye-dazzling descriptions of war and of tournaments."

Waverley's father, hoping to provide his dreamy son with some discipline and direction, obtains for him a commission in a military regiment stationed in Dundee, on Scotland's east coast. On the way there, however, Edward decides to visit the Baron of Bradwardine, one of his uncle's old friends. As he approaches the Baron's estate, close to the Highland line, Waverley enters "the straggling village, or rather hamlet, of Tully-Veolan," which Scott renders with considerable realistic detail. The houses seem "miserable in the extreme, especially to an eye accustomed to the smiling neatness of English cottages." The people themselves look intelligent if grave, and "from among the young women, an artist might have chosen more than one model, whose features and form resembled those of Minerva."

Despite their physical attractions, however, the people of Tully-Veolan appear to have been stuck in a semi-feudal backwater, untouched by the light of British civilization. The streets are unpaved and filled with a score of barking dogs. The people are badly-dressed, worn out. The lovely village girls, shabbily clad, could have been considerably improved "by a plentiful application of spring water, with a *quantum sufficit* of soap."

Such stepping-back by the narrator for an ironic touch of comic observation is plentiful in *Waverley*; Scott was a great admirer of Henry Fielding, who similarly packed his novels with amusing portraits of recognizably eccentric types. The Baron of Bradwardine is "no bad representative of the old school." He sports an "embroidered coat, and superbly barred waistcoat," and a "brigadier wig, surmounted by a small gold-laced cocked-hat." He maintains his crumbling estate near the hills where ancient clans of Celtic-speaking, kilt-wearing Highlanders maintain the practices and traditions that have sustained them for centuries. Unlike Edward, Brad-wardine is "upright, starched, and stoical."

The baron, however, has a lovely daughter, Rose, who is somewhat younger than Edward, "a girl scarce seventeen," who looks to the oddly ed-ucated Englishman for instruction and counsel. At this point in the novel, Edward thinks of Rose Bradwardine as a "beautiful and amiable" younger sister, the "playful little girl, who now asked Edward to mend her pen, now to construe a stanza in Tasso, and now how to spell a very, very long word in her version of it." She has not quite the sort of "beauty or merit" that might make her the object of Edward's affections. He was, after all, a "youth of imagination" and wanted a woman before whom he would "bow" and "tremble," someone "to adore."

Initially, Edward is granted a leave of absence from his commanding officer, who nonetheless warns him in a letter of dallying for too long "with persons, who, estimable as they might be in a general sense, could not be supposed well affected to a government which they declined to acknowledge by taking the oath of allegiance." The "letter further insinuated, though with great delicacy, that although some family connections might be supposed to render it necessary for Captain Waverley to communicate with gentlemen who were in this unpleasant state of suspicion, yet his father's situation and wishes ought to prevent his prolonging those attentions into exclusive inti-macy. And it was intimated, that while his political principles were endan-gered by communicating with laymen of this description, he might also receive erroneous impressions in religion from the prelatic clergy, who so perversely laboured to set up the royal prerogative in things sacred."

The longer Waverley stays at Tully-Veolan, the more enamored he be-comes of Highland ways. Through Bradwardine, Waverley meets the Mac-Ivor clan, and its leader, Fergus—described by Rose as "a very polite, handsome man"—who spent much of his youth in France, where he culti-vated ties to the exiled Stuart family and shared their dream of returning a Catholic king, a Stuart, to the English throne. Fergus, Rose adds, is "the Chieftain of an independent branch of a powerful Highland clan." He is "much respected, both for his own power, and that of his kith, kin, and al-lies." Fergus, in fact, is the consummate Highland chief, tending closely to the care and feeding of his own household and those of his tribe, who ap-pear at turns gracious and suspicious, brave and barbarous.

When Waverley attends a great feast on Fergus's estate, the liquor flows. The "bagpipers, three in number, screamed, during the whole time of dinner, a tremendous war-tune; and the echoing of the vaulted roof, and clang of the Celtic tongue, produced such a Babel of noises, that Waverley dreaded his ears would never recover it." The central dish, "a yearling lamb, called 'a hog in har'st,'" was roasted whole, and "set upon its legs, with a bunch of parsley in its mouth, and probably exhibited in that form to gratify the pride of the cook, who piqued himself more on the plenty than the elegance of his master's table." As Edward looks on: "the sides of this poor animal were fiercely attacked by the clansmen, some with dirks, others with knives which were usually in the same sheath with the dagger, so that it was soon rendered a mangled and rueful spectacle."

Such scenes foreshadow the bloody violence to come. In one of the novel's more celebrated chapters, Edward takes part in a stag-hunt with Fergus and "about three hundred of his clan, well armed, and accoutered in their best fashion." The event signals Waverley's own initiation into the clan, for he has accommodated his new friends by putting on "the trews (he could not be reconciled to the kilt), brogues, and bonnet, as the fittest dress for the exercise in which he was to be engaged, and which least exposed to be stared at as a stranger when they should reach the place of rendezvous."

The chiefs and their men proceed to drive the deer together, their efforts assisted by packs of baying dogs. The deer are plentiful, and the "fattest" ones are shot; but some, "the tallest of the red-deer stags," arrange themselves "in a sort of battle-array, gazing on the group which barred their passage down the glen." In desperation they charge, and Waverley, missing the Gaelic command to hit the ground, is nearly flattened by the charging herd. Fergus saves Waverley, pulling him "with violence to the ground." Waverley sustains "several very severe contusions" and a sprained ankle, and he is promptly deposited in a "wigwam" on "a couch of heather." He is attended by "a surgeon, or he who assumed the office, appeared to unite the characters of a leech and a conjuror." This medicine man, "an old smoke-dried Highlander," ceremoniously approaches Edward, "making the *deasil*," which involves circling "his couch three times, moving from east to west, according to the course of the sun." Then, muttering "gibberish," he treats Edwards with an "embrocation" of boiled herbs. "The fomentation had had a speedy effect in alleviating the pain and swelling, which our hero imputed to the virtue of the herbs, or the effect of the chafing, but which by the by-standers unanimously ascribed to the spells with which the operation had been accompanied."

Bit by bit, Edward is embraced by Fergus's tribe, with Fergus now clearly supporting Bonnie Prince Charlie, who slips into Scotland from Italy by way of France to assert once more his family's claim to the throne. Charles—the "Young Chevalier," quietly backed by some prominent English Tories and the French King, Louis XV—believes he can cultivate the anti-Hanoverian sentiments that still simmer in the Highlands. Meanwhile, Fergus has per-suaded himself that, with the help of his Highland warriors, Prince Charles' quest will be a success; that a series of speedy military victories against gov-ernment forces will inevitably rally more supporters to the Stuart side.

Fergus also assumes that those supporting the Prince will be "raised to honour and rank," and his motives are fueled by self-interest: A "future coronet" glitters before his eyes. Fergus, then, is cunning and manipulative, as Edward eventually discovers; he can also be gratuitously cruel. Edward had "been more than once shocked at the small degree of sympathy which Fergus exhibited for the feelings even of those whom he loved, if they did not correspond with his own mood at the time and more especially if they thwarted him while earnest in a favorite pursuit." Fergus wants Edward Waverley on the Stuart side, for recruiting him will, he knows, prove highly popular with the Young Chevalier.

Thus Fergus encourages Edward's attraction to his sister Flora, who is no less devoted to "the cause of making James Stewart a king," and who (according to Rose Braderwine) "is one of the most beautiful and accom-plished young ladies in this country." "I must tell you," Fergus tells Flora, "that Captain Waverley is a worshipper of the Celtic muse, not the less so perhaps that he does not understand a word of her language." And so Flora, this "fair Highland damsel," duly lures Waverley, "like a knight of romance," into a picturesque glen, which opens "into a land of romance": "a sylvan ampitheatre, waving with birch, young oaks, and hazels." The nearby hills are "purple with heath." There is a "romantic waterfall" before which Flora positions herself, the better to be savored by Waverley's riveted gaze. "Never, even in his wildest dreams," Scott reports, "had Edward imagined such a beautiful woman, looking for all the world like a fair enchantress of

Boijardo or Ariosto, by whose nod the scenery seemed to have been created, an Eden in the wilderness."

Against this backdrop Flora lifts her harp and launches into a "lofty and uncommon air," which had been "a battle-song in former ages." Edward swoons. He "would not for worlds have quitted his place at her side." Yet he also finds himself longing for solitude, the better to "decipher and examine at leisure the complications of motives which now agitated his bosom."

For Edward, these complications have consequences. He is, after all, an Englishman, the son of a prominent Whig. And because he has failed to join his English regiment, the charge of desertion hangs over his head. Thus, in his more clear-headed moments, Edward realizes that flirting with the MacIvors and their dream of the Stuart restoration is folly. James the Second, after all, had forfeited his crown in 1688. "Since that period, four monarchs had reigned in peace and glory over Britain, sustaining and exalting the character of the nation abroad, and its liberties at home. Reason asked, was it worth while to disturb government so long settled and established, and to plunge a kingdom into all the miseries of civil war, for the purpose of replacing upon the throne the descendants of a monarch by whom it had been willfully forfeited?"

Still, Waverley lingers in the Highlands, and he even consorts with the Prince Charles himself, who appears briefly in *Waverley* as a dashing but surprisingly modest young man moving comfortably among Fergus's warriors, unfailingly confident in the victory of his righteous cause. Of course, the Young Pretender is also eager to have Waverley in his battalion, and so flatters him with by telling Fergus that "no master of ceremonies is necessary to present a Waverley to a Stewart." "I desire to gain no adherents save from affection and conviction," he graciously adds, assuring Waverley that he is free to return home if he likes and even to join the forces of George II.

Edward swoons again: "Unaccustomed to the address and manners of a polished court, in which Charles was eminently skillful, his words and his kindness penetrated the heart of our hero, and easily outweighed all prudential motives." Waverley was "irresistibly attracted to the cause which the prejudices of education, and the political principles of his family, had already recommended as the most just."

Not surprisingly, the romantic Waverley throws his support to the Young Chevalier. And initially, at least, it appears that the Second Jacobite Rising will succeed. At Prestonpans, near Edinburgh, Prince Charles and his allies draw up a precise plan for their first serious encounter with government troops.

Before the battle, Edward finds himself agitated once more. He fancies himself loyal to Fergus and, more to the point, to the divine Flora. He now wears Highlander garb. But he is also aware that he will soon be fighting an English cavalry whose standard he recognizes. In the distance, he can hear his own tongue spoken by a commanding officer, Colonel Gardiner, "for whom he had once felt so much respect." "It was at that instant, that, looking around him, he saw the wild dress and appearance of his Highland associates, heard their whispers in an uncouth and unknown language, looked upon his own dress, so unlike that which he had worn from infancy, and wished to awake from what seemed at the moment a dream, strange, horrible, and unnatural. 'Good God!' he muttered, 'am I then a traitor to my country, a renegade to my standard, and a foe . . . to my native England!'"

The Highlanders execute a surprise attack at dawn, charging out of the mist with swords drawn and bagpipes blaring. The English infantrymen, Scott carefully notes, at first "stood their ground with great courage." But, overwhelmed, they flee, terrified at the sight of Highlanders "furious and eager for spoil." Colonel Gardiner—like Prince Charles, a real historical figure placed briefly within the novel's action—fights on gallantly, "spurring his horse through the field," despite "his clothes and saddle being marked with blood." Waverley tries to save "this good and brave man," but the officer is cut from his horse "by the blow of a scythe." On the ground, as Waverley looks on, Gardiner receives "more wounds than would let out twenty lives." Worse, "the dying warrior seemed to recognize Edward, for he fixed his eye upon him with an upbraiding, yet sorrowful look, and appeared to struggle for utterance."

Scott, however, is careful to limit his description of Waverley's participation in battle. After all, the Jacobites will lose, and the rule of the Hanoverians will prevail; it would make no sense for the hero of Scott's first historical novel to be shown slaughtering English soldiers in the service of a traitorous cause. In fact, Edward's main role in battle appears to be saving English officers from harm. As John Sutherland suggests, Waverley "wanders through the battlefield offering as little danger to his foe as a dormouse in a tiger's cage." Scott's "remarkably patchy and vague" description of the battle at Prestonpans is deliberate: The author wants to imply that Edward was valorous, but he cannot show him fighting and killing his countrymen.

Does Waverley actually kill any Englishmen? Does he even draw English blood? The Chevalier himself, Scott tells us, "paid him many compliments on his distinguished bravery." And Fergus adds, "Your behaviour is praised by every living person, to the skies." "All our beauties of the white rose are pulling caps for you." But for what? "Had Scott not faded out the battlefield details," Sutherland notes, "it would be very difficult to tolerate Waverley's surviving so comfortably." For "either Edward Waverley is the most incompetent warrior who ever lived or—still bearing the King's commission—he killed the King's men."

Throughout, Scott implies in *Waverley* that Edward's attachment to Highland Scotland was entirely unmoored and emotional, tied to the color of their customs and the charms of Flora MacIvor. Inevitably, then, Edward Waverley returns to reason and acceptance of the political order that Scott himself endorsed. When Edward finally breaks with the Jacobites, Scott writes that he "felt himself entitled to say firmly, though perhaps with a sigh, that the romance of his life was ended, and that its real history had now commenced."

That new life will not include Flora, who enters a convent in France. Nor will it include a continuation of his tense friendship with Fergus, who is captured and beheaded, but not before bellowing "God save King *James!*" Instead, Edward marries Rose Braderwine and helps her family financially, even commissioning a "large and spirited painting" that is hung prominently in the Baron's home at Tully-Veolan. It shows Fergus MacIvor and Waverley "in their Highland dress, the scene a wild, rocky, and mountainous pass, down which the clan were descending in the background." Moreover, "Beside this painting hung the arms which Waverley had borne in the unfortunate civil war. The whole piece was beheld with admiration, and deeper feelings."

The shrewd Flora saw it coming. She rebuffed Edward's affections, the novel strongly implies, because she recognized that he was too much an

Englishman—too thoroughly embedded in the modern Protestant world of commerce, individualism, and economic striving—ever really to embrace the values and interests values of her Catholic, Gaelic-speaking tribe. In fact, Flora foresees that Edward Waverley would become Walter Scott, drawn more to books than to battles, settled in the stately prosperity of the Tory gentry, cultivating an interest in the symbols and tokens of a lost and idealized world.

"He will be at home," Flora rightly predicts, "in the quiet circle of domestic happiness, lettered indolence, and elegant enjoyments, of Waverley-Honour. And he will refit the old library in the most exquisite Gothic taste, and garnish its shelves with the rarest and most valuable volumes;— and he will draw plans and landscapes, and write verses, and rear temples, and dig grottoes;—and he will stand in a clear summer night in the colonnade before the hall, and gaze on the deer as they stray in the moonlight, or lie shadowed by the boughs of the huge old fantastic oaks;—and he will repeat verses to his beautiful wife, who will hang upon his arm; and he will be a happy man."

V

Out of all this came . . . well, what? Walter Scott had a surprisingly realistic prose style, and that style could be traced through innumerable later authors in the history of the novel. Tolstoy learned his realism, in a sterner form, probably from Stendhal, but he could have extracted it from its nascent presence in a historical setting in *Waverley*. Scott had, as well, a full indulgence of Romanticism's notion that deep feeling is the true sign of an authentic self. Those historical doorstoppers of Alexandre Dumas's *Three Musketeers* novels (1844–1850) obviously do not happen without Scott's model, but neither, in a sense, does Victor Hugo's turn to Romantic medievalism with *The Hunchback of Notre-Dame* (1831) or the near-history anti-Romantic Romanticism of Stendhal's *The Charterhouse of Parma* (1839). And the strange perfection of the combination of that realistic and Romantic prose in Robert Louis Stevenson (along with the deliberate writing of it in children's stories) owes more to Scott than just Stevenson's shared origin in Scotland.

Still, it is neither his realism nor his Romanticism that makes us look to Sir Walter Scott for the origin of something particular in the modern novel—the origin of something that we do not quite find in Sophia Lee's 1783 *The Recess* or Jane Porter's 1803 *Thaddeus of Warsaw* or any other of the early examples of historical settings in fiction, however enjoyable or unreadable we now find those novels. Scott is both revealing a cultural problem and suggesting its solution in *Waverley*. In the wonderful implausibility of taking a modern psyche and casting it by time-travel into a premodern world, Scott is using the near-past of Scotland to show readers what they lack in modern Britain. At the same time, in the novel's happy conclusion, he offers what he imagines is the way to reconcile the modern hunger for a thick world with modern advances in knowledge about both the self and the external world.

Edward does at last accept the modern world in *Waverley*, just as in the end he marries Rose Bradwardine rather than Flora MacIvor. (As so often in Scott, the hero ends up with the beautiful and faithful blonde instead of the beautiful and passionate brunette by whom he had been tempted; is it really any surprise that Italian opera would be drawn to Scott's stories?) But Edward entered the premodern world precisely because it contained what modernity did not. The Scotland that Walter Scott pictures as fighting with Bonnie Prince Charles is a place filled with emotion, of course. Scott is at least partially a Romantic, after all. But Scott's Scotland is able to have that emotional texture because it is thick with things properly demanding emotion—rich with things broadcasting their dense meaning to Edward: family, historical continuity, oaths, royalty, the dramatic scenery of an untamed countryside, etc.

If all that can inspire a woman as passionate as Flora, how could her beauty not join with the rest to inspire Edward Waverley? This is, after all, what he lacks. What all of Britain lacks. The modern world is disenchanted, and the sentimental soul feels the absence of objects calling to it. This is where the historical novel as a genre joins with the Gothic novel and the novel of sentiment. All of them feel the problem of the isolation of the soul, cast into a thin world without objects worthy of its passions.

The defeat of the Jacobites is not presented by Scott as unalloyed tragedy, and Edward does find happiness at the novel's end. A good modern, writing a modern novel in a historical setting, Scott casts his modern character back into the past. But his purpose—the solution he thinks he has found—is actually the reverse: to draw the past into the present. With historical memory in the objects that Edward collects (as Scott himself did at his home in Abbotsford), he argues that knowledge of the past, a feeling of connection to it, can allow us to advance as moderns without suffering the worst effects of modern isolation in the universe.

Walter Scott was wrong—as Gogol was wrong. Museums would prove insufficient devices for keeping modernity from further thinning the world, and objects intrinsically worthy of human sentiment would seem fewer and fewer as the years went by. But Scott saw the problem. We have to give him that. And he tried, at least, to find an answer.

CHAPTER 6 | CHARLES DICKENS AND THE TRUTH

I

Never was there such a book as *David Copperfield* for the giving of names, and the changing of names, and the just plain getting wrong of names. David himself is called by dozens of names in the course of the novel—indeed, the novel is almost defined by the fact that nearly every character in it uses a distinct name for the boy (as Norman Talbot and Donald Hawes pointed out in a pair of seminal articles back in 1978).

But David is not alone in having multiple names. All the characters in *David Copperfield* pass under more than one name. Richard Babley is called Mr. Dick to his face, and Mrs. Markleham called the Old Soldier behind her back. Steerforth is misremembered as Rudderford, and Ham Peggotty mispronounced as Am, "a morsel of English Grammar." Betsey Trotwood calls the murderous Murdstone "Murderer" and the jelly-lipped Chillip "Jellips," but Betsey herself has arbitrarily resumed her maiden name. Barkis hides his wealth under the name Blackboy, while Micawber hides his poverty under Mortimer. Uriah Heep ends as model prisoner Twenty-Seven, Peggotty marries to become C.P. Barkis, the serving-girl Clickett dubs herself the Orfling, and even the long-mislaid schoolmaster Mr. Mell makes a curtain call as Doctor Mell.

Names always fascinate characters in Dickens's novels. Bumble explains over gin the alphabetical system with which he "invented" Oliver Twist; Nicholas Nickleby refuses to believe a woman named "Bobster" could be his love; Mr. Gradgrind in *Hard Times* declares "Sissy is not a name" immediately upon hearing it. But the fascination in *David Copperfield* goes far beyond that in the other novels. Betsey Trotwood blusters into Blunderstone Rookery in the opening pages and promptly scorns the name of the house, disparages the name of the servant, and proposes for the unborn child the most unlikely name of the three. In his dramatic confrontation with Uriah Heep, Micawber not only scores off Uriah's name, but introduces Mr. Dick as "Dixon"—and foolish Mr. Dick pauses to weigh his new name. The narrating David turns aside repeatedly to speak of names. At his most facetious, he remarks on the names in Doctors' Commons; at his most pathetic, he comments on the name above a shop on the Dover road.

In part, this heightened fascination is possible because names in *David Copperfield* are unlike names in the earlier novels. Perhaps Dickens learned something from naming *Nicholas Nickleby*'s Lord Verisopht, whom he began satirically but had subsequently to make sympathetic. Or perhaps the difference is forced upon him by first-person narration, for *Great Expectations* also seems mostly to have names unlike those in the early novels (though the alternating chapters in *Bleak House* narrated by Esther in the first person do not).

But in *David Copperfield*, the names are not a joke between author and reader from which the characters are excluded. Dickens has let his characters in on their naming, and a richness and subtlety of names results. The broad humor of a pettifogger named Fogg and a nag named Knag, of Jingle and Humm and Snobb and Curdle, of an undertaker named Mould and another named Sowerberry, is too cruel to impose on characters who are conscious of their own names, and Dickens mostly leaves it behind. There are exceptions in *David Copperfield*, of course, as Dickens could never resist a jab at a schoolmaster, and the names of Creakle, Sharp, Mell, and Tungay are throwbacks to the humor of "Wackford Squeers" and "Doctor Blimber." But in general *David Copperfield* avoids the in-joke of unconscious names.

The unconscious names, however, soon reappear. *Bleak House*, Dickens's next novel, is a festival of cruel but funny names. This reappearance, when taken with the multiple names for the characters in *David Copperfield* and those characters unceasing fascination with names, suggests Dickens has a program in mind for naming in *David Copperfield*. The tension between meaning and reference—the curious fact of language, using *this* word for *that* thing—is translated into the story itself. The characters themselves feel the tension of naming and explore together with the author what their names are for.

They find first much what we would expect them to find. The order of names—the hierarchy of terms by which the characters refer to and address one another—betrays the power and desire that stand behind the screens of politeness and grammatical necessity. As he grows, David must overcome every attempt to name him: Murdstone's disinheriting "David," Micawber's premature "Copperfield," Steerforth's diminishing "Daisy," Dora's cloying "Doady." Even Betsey Trotwood proposes to rename him upon his arrival in Dover (though Mr. Dick, as the baptismal father who washes, robes, and names the boy, interprets her proposal as a given name rather than a patronym). And just as David finds sanctuary near Canterbury Cathedral from the destruction Murdstone intended for him in London, so he finds sanctuary in "Trotwood" from the hurt Murdstone had done to "David." But he must at last overcome even his new-christened name to reclaim his usurped patrimony.

Dickens and his characters find more, however, than that a name expresses and enforces the desire of the namer. Certainly, names in *David Copperfield* have a way of coming true: David's mother blunders and brings the murdering Murdstone to Blunderstone; David's father may have called his house the Rookery "when there's not a rook near it," but with the Murdstones, dressed in black, the rooks have come; the lamb Agnes Wick*field* at last marries Copper*field*, after being struggled over by a David and a Uriah, just as Bathsheba was. This is the threat of "Towzer" and "Master Murdstone," proposed names that David dodges in the course of the novel: A boy called Towzer will become a dog and a boy called Murdstone will become a stone of *merde*, just as—to take a pair of names David doesn't dodge—a young man called Daisy must be seduced and a grown man called Doady ("a corruption of David") must behave like a child. Extrinsic denomination, borrowing from scholastic philosophy a phrase for naming by relation, has a way of becoming intrinsic denomination, of becoming true of the person apart from any relation to the namer.

The possibility of names coming true, however, requires there be such a thing as truth, just as an observation of the failure of extrinsic names requires there be an alternative of intrinsic names against which to measure that failure. An analogy might make this clearer. *David Copperfield*, Dickens's only book with a writer as its hero, contains a serious attack on writing. The novel mocks the extravagance of Julia's diary and Micawber's letters as well as Dr. Strong's impossible dictionary, Mr. Dick's interrupted memorial, Dora's indecipherable housekeeping book, Traddles's unwritten letters to his uncle, and Spenlow's feigned will. But Dickens is not indulging some complicated and ironic self-critique. By mocking bad writing, he looks rather to defend the possibility of good writing.

Similarly, by indicting the abuse of names, the novel looks to demonstrate not only the abusive power of false names, but the possibility of true names as well. No one has ever accused Dickens of being a philosopher. But *David Copperfield* offers us an opportunity for thinking philosophically about naming. Dickens shows how a name imposed in the economy of power and desire pushes a person into an expression of that name. He also shows, however, how the real essence to which a true name refers pushes back on that economy with the moral force of truth.

II

By the time the art form of the novel reaches Charles Dickens in 1850, many of its social purposes had come clear, particularly in the battle against poverty. Many of its moral purposes were clear as well, particularly in the long Victorian denunciation of hypocrisy. But in the line we have identified throughout this study of the novel, the line of the Protestant-inflected self that must somehow understand its justification—in every sense of the word but especially the biblical—and move toward the sanctification demanded by its ideal truth, the cultural purposes of the novel were not so obvious.

The twentieth century's desire to see everything through Marxist or post-Marxist lenses (economic class, race, gender) makes it difficult for us to understand that Western civilization's cultural problems then, as now, originate in a metaphysical crisis. The clarity achieved by the modern self— in its Protestantism, among the other elective affinities that Weber insisted had joined to give us modernity—was purchased at the price of a thick supernatural order.

In the last chapter, we looked at a novelist's efforts to present and solve the problem with the genre of the historical novel, and Dickens himself would write two historical novels, *Barnaby Rudge* (1841) and *A Tale of Two Cities* (1859). But the metaphysical crisis was too large to be addressed quite so easily. The world had grown even thinner between Walter Scott in 1814 and Dickens in 1850. The novel of sentiment increasingly failed in the decline of the plausibility of objects broadcasting their demand for deep feeling. And as for the self, its novelistic path became more difficult, as the outer representation, the hero's journey, of the interior path, the hero's salvation and sanctification, required that the world be charged with meaning. And who could believe that, in the absence of a perceived supernatural influence on the objects around us?

It falls to Dickens—the great unconscious genius of the age, the towering figure of the Victorian novel—to express the problem in terms of truth. If David Copperfield can discern his true name, then there is such a thing as truth. And thus language, which is, after all, a novelist's only tool, has the capacity to link the interior of the self to the exterior world. The journey within the self would again be reflected by journey of the body through external space, and the art form of the novel could again not merely present but also *solve* the cultural crisis of the age.

III

Victorian English prized rhetorical variation and provided an enormous set of vocatives and nominatives for reference and address. Characters in *David Copperfield* are called by title ("Doctor"), surname ("Traddles"), title and surname ("Mr. Murdstone"), Christian name ("Dora"), title and Christian name ("Master David"), title and both names ("Mr. Wilkins Micawber"), title and husband's name ("Mrs. David Copperfield"), and Christian name and both surnames ("Clara Peggotty Barkis"); by polite sign ("Ma'am"), ignorance marker ("What's-your-name"), and grammatical person ("You"). They have nicknames formed as diminutives ("Ury"), shortenings ("Tom"), and corruptions ("Doady"), and nonce-names taken directly from substance ("Man") or drawn metonymically from an accidental category: relation ("Aunt"), action ("Driver"), passion ("Dear"), possession ("Red Whisker"), location ("Londoner"), quality ("Young Innocence"), etc. Any of these may be subject to further metonymy ("Yarmouth Bloater"), metaphor ("Mealy Potatoes"), allusion ("Croesus"), or comic reversal ("Six-foot" for a three-foot child).

We come to expect this variety, for it saves us from the weariness of repetition and matches our experience—an experience formed by rhetorical variation. And when we meet repetition, as when Uriah Heep calls David "Master Copperfield" twenty-three times in forty-two sentences, we know *something* (whether comic or serious) has occurred.

And yet, although Victorian variation is wide, it is not unlimited. No finite language can express completely the infinite distinctions among beings. (No finite language can express completely even a *single* distinction, for that matter.) But each language expresses most fully those distinctions in which its speakers are most interested—or at least were once interested, since language is often conservative and preserves vocabularies for distinctions long after the social necessity for those distinctions is gone. Victorian modes of reference and address express distinctions of (and thus reveal interest in) gender, age, education, marriage, family relation, military rank, priesthood, ownership of land, occupation, formality of the occasion, mood of the speaker, and many other things besides. But, most of all, names in Victorian English express fine degrees of social status and personal affection—of rank and sentiment.

A world of linguistic convention is revealed the moment David first speaks aloud: "'Peggotty,' says I suddenly, 'were you ever married?' 'Lord, Master Davy,' replied Peggotty. 'What's put marriage in your head?'"

The fact that the language has titles for distinguishing married women from unmarried women betrays an interest its speakers take in the distinction. And yet, while David's mother keeps "Mrs." in her widowhood, Betsey Trotwood resumes "Miss" despite her marriage, and titles are often omitted anyway, as Peggotty's is. More, the contrast of the marriage titles "Miss" and "Mrs." is corrupted by the contrast between the age and status vocatives "Miss" and "Ma'am." "Don't *Missis* me, ma'am," screeches the enraged Fanny Squeers when called "child" by her newly married contemporary 'Tilda in *Nicholas Nickleby*. Victorian English imperfectly distinguishes married from unmarried women, and David's confusion about Peggotty's marriage is possible in the language.

No confusion is possible, however, about rank and sentiment. Peggotty is well loved, but just as Polly Toodle is called "Richards" in *Dombey and Son* merely for her employer's convenience and the servant Harriet Beadle insulted with "Tattycoram" in *Little Dorrit*, so Peggotty's name reveals her rank in *David Copperfield*: "'Do you mean to say, child,' [asked Betsey,] 'that any human being has gone into a Christian church and gotten herself named Peggotty?' 'It's her surname,' said my mother faintly. 'Mr. Copperfield called her by it, because her Christian name was the same as mine.'"

An untitled surname implies at least equality. So David uses surnames with his schoolmates, and Micawber (taking the boy as an equal and thus someone for whom he need not be responsible) quickly comes to call him "Copperfield." The child David's use of "Peggotty," however, reveals both that he feels close to her and that his rank outweighs a child's conventional inferiority to an adult. And Peggotty's "Master Davy," a diminutive with a title, reveals the same relation from the other side: a close affection and a social gap.

Dickens does more, however, than echo the existing order of names. He shows the way in which, precisely because names mark degrees of rank and sentiment, names are available for the assertion of power and desire. In the closed world of Blunderstone Rookery, no one uses the Christian name mistress and servant share. But by concealing from the reader a name the narrator could have revealed, Dickens creates a mystery that makes the revelation more dramatic. We do not hear the name until Murdstone uses it to admonish his new wife for showing affection to her son, and this admonishment frames David's memory of his mother's remarriage. The novel reveals "Clara" in the first sentence the boy hears upon seeing his newly married mother and "Clara" is the last word he hears as he leaves her forever. Murdstone's use of Clara's Christian name illustrates the new order in the Rookery as clearly as do his first words to Peggotty:

> "My friend," turning a darkening face on Peggotty, when he had watched my mother out, and dismissed her with a nod and a smile: "Do you know your mistress's name? . . . I thought I heard you, as I came upstairs, call her by a name [viz., Mrs. Copperfield] that is not hers. She has taken mine, you know. Will you remember that?"

Murdstone neither lies to David and Peggotty nor speaks in an unconventional way. Husbands in Victorian novels generally call their wives by Christian names; wives in Victorian novels generally take their husbands' surnames. But truth and convention are only accidentally in Murdstone's mouth. The man is a perverter of language (as he is of religion) because he uses grammatical necessity—the necessity to refer and address by *some* distinction—as a tool of desire. He uses naming not to name but to assert his power to name:

"It's very hard," said my mother, "that in my own house—"

"*My* own house?" repeated Mr. Murdstone. "Clara!"

"*Our* own house, I mean," faltered my mother, evidently fright-
ened—"I hope you know what I mean, Edward—it's very hard
that in *your* own house I may not have a word to say."

Throughout *David Copperfield*, Dickens uses naming to show rank and
sentiment. David's schoolmasters employ his Christian name only in sympathy for his mother's death. "Little Gent" maintains a space around David
at the warehouse, and he is called nothing personal except when he recounts
some story to entertain the older men. In meeting David as an adult, Miss
Murdstone refuses to grant him the status of "Mr." and is left with the oddity of addressing him by his whole name, "David Copperfield"—just as Mr.
Wickfield (once Uriah Heep has grown great) repeatedly refers to his former clerk by both Christian name and surname.

Throughout the novel, Dickens uses the perversion of naming to expose power and desire. Murdstone is the type, but he is not alone. Creakle
mocks Mell's poverty with "Mr. What's-your-name," only to become furious
when the dismissed teacher does not use an employer's title in reply: "Sir,
to you!" Creakle screams. Uriah Heep is clever, and his repeated "Master
Copperfield,—I mean Mister Copperfield" is a wonderfully witty abuse of
language. Miss Murdstone has flashes of this sort of abusive wit ("Generally
speaking," she says, "I don't like boys. How d'ye do, boy?"), and Miss Mow-
cher is also good at wicked name-play, as when she signals with the nam-
ing-game of Forfeits that she understands her role in procuring Emily. Even
the sponger and would-be seducer Jack Maldon, with his "I call him the
old Doctor—it's all the same you know," and the pandering Littimer, with
his respectable lack of a Christian name and refusal of superlatives, pervert
the order of names. All the villains in *David Copperfield* abuse language.

III

That all villains abuse language, however, does not necessarily mean that
all who abuse language are villains. If the villainous characters use words
to twist reality, there are nonetheless comic characters who take words
themselves as real. The grim Murdstone stands on one side of *David*

Copperfield. But standing on the other, like laughter holding both his sides, is Wilkins Micawber.

Or perhaps all abusers of language *are* villains. Generous motives and innocuous consequences mark the moral characters in Dickens's early novels. Everyone tells stories in the *Pickwick Papers*, but Jingle wants to help himself and Pickwick wants to help others; Job Trotter hurts people and Sam Weller does not. By this standard, Mr. Micawber is a villain. He is comic and congenial, larger than the life that jails him for his debts: He is Pickwick and Weller loosened a notch, and his manipulation of language can make a nondescript house a theater, a ruined dinner a feast, and debtors' prison a carnival. But he is also Jingle and Trotter tightened a notch, for he hurts people along the way. It is not really funny that the bootmaker wants to be paid and the milkman needs his money. Micawber may at last redeem himself, but only after helping destroy Wickfield. Traddles, scrimping for marriage, has his furniture confiscated to pay Micawber's debts. Mr. Micawber does have some "moral (or rather immoral) resemblance" to Murdstone and Heep.

Of course, we join David in exempting Micawber from condemnation as a villain. And there is a moral difference, for he is never systematically cruel—as Murdstone is in beating David to train Clara, as Heep is in robbing Betsey to ruin David. Micawber has the virtue of his vices and is as incapable of systematic harm as he is of systematic thrift. Indeed, he has an openness Murdstone, Heep, and Creakle (with his "system" of silent prison discipline) could never know. Micawber is not selfish, but only absorbed in the drama of himself, and when he meets a real villain in Heep, he loses the dramatic power of words that is his charm for living.

Similarly, we join David in exempting Micawber from condemnation as a liar. An enormous amount of dishonesty occurs in *David Copperfield*. A wicked character like Heep is obviously a forger and a systematic liar. But everyone in the novel indulges falsity. The fly-drivers in Dover lie to David, the inveiglers in Doctors' Commons lie to clients, and the servants David and Dora hire lie to everyone. In sorting out Heep's chicanery, Traddles discovers not only that Wickfield has fraudulently remitted interest while aware of the loss of capital, but that Betsey has lied about her destitution (just as she twice pushes David toward Agnes with a "pious fraud"). Traddles himself practices a naive subterfuge to redeem his flower-stand, Steerforth misleads his mother, and Barkis shams poverty. The lie Mr. Spenlow tells about having made his will may be excusable— "there is no subject on which men are so inconsistent," his clerk Tiffy declares, "and so little to be trusted"—but dishonesty is Spenlow's defining trait: He lies about his wealth, methodically misrepresents the temperament of his partner Jorkins, and defends the Commons on the grounds appearance is as good as truth.

Young David is a liar, too. "If you make a brag of your honesty," a tinker threatens on the road to Dover, "I'll knock your brains out," and David has no right to brag: He lies about his name on his birthday in London, tells the Orfling fantastic stories, and deceives Peggotty in a money-begging letter. "Never be false," Betsey advises him, but nine pages later he lies to Uriah about Betsey herself. David's anxiety of "imposture" at Dr. Strong's is finally the fear of being found out false—a fear that resurfaces after his drunken dissipation: "I could scarcely lay claim to the name. . . . However, I told [the ticket-porter] that I was T. Copperfield, Esquire, and he believed it." Lies constantly tempt David: in the flurried thought of asking at Mr. Mills's door for Mr. Blackboy, in the dishonorable correspondence with Dora, even in his fiction-writing. "Your being secret and clandestine, is not being like yourself," Agnes admonishes him, "in the candor of your nature."

And yet, Micawber's lies are somehow different. The interminable sentences and linguistic gestures, the synonymizing and circumlocution, are comic because Micawber creates not himself but language—because he sets words free. A lie typically strains language: It is just as constrained by truth as honesty is, and constrained further by the liar's desire for truth to be other than it is. Dickens shows with Micawber, however, a lying that frees rather than strains language. Micawber does not speak ungrammatically or nonsensically, but grammar and meaning are all the constraint his words admit. Language in Micawber's mouth is released from the necessity to express its speaker's desire, to conform to truth, even to convince its hearers. Each phrase suggests not what next to say but a synonymous inflation of what he has already said. His circumlocution is not avoidance but inflation: a turning of words back on themselves.

Dickens's use of irony shows this same free play of words. There is some complicated verbal irony in *David Copperfield*, but Micawber's speech has the simple irony of comic hypocrisy: such truths from such a source.

"Annual income twenty pounds, annual expenditure nineteen nineteen six, result happiness," the extravagant debtor happily informs David. "Never do tomorrow what you can do today," he advises. "Procrastination is the thief of time. Collar him!"—but Micawber *is* Procrastination, wearing an imposing collar and collared in the King's Bench prison. Even when he speaks the truth, the irony of his saying something true puts his words above their truth. Language finds in Micawber a nearly perfect medium through which to speak itself, for he wears language as he wears his quizzing-glass: "for ornament, as I afterwards found, as he very seldom looked through it, and couldn't see anything when he did."

Dickens consistently exploits abused language for comedy. Even with Betsey Trotwood's willful errors set aside, the novel is full of confusions about words. "A Baboo—or a Begum" is misremembered by Mrs. Copperfield as a "baboon," "crocodiles" misunderstood by Peggotty as vegetable "crorkindills," "sweethearts" misheard by David as "sweetmeats," "Doctor" misread by Mrs. Markleham as "Proctor," "jury" mispronounced by Mrs. Crupp as "judy," and "elements" misspoken by Micawber as "elephants." Mrs. Crupp calls her lodger "Copperfull," "firstly, no doubt, because it was not my name; and secondly, I am inclined to think, in some indistinct association with a washing-day."

And Dickens consistently shows the moral ambiguity of comic characters. Micawber is the type, but he is not alone. Mrs. Markleham is a comically ceaseless talker—"What a useful work a Dictionary is!" she declares, "What a necessary work! The meaning of words! Without Doctor Johnson . . . we might have been at this present moment calling an Italian-iron a bedstead"—but she nearly destroys the Strongs by forcing her notion of their marriage upon them.

Similarly, Julia Mills has a "wonderful flow of words," and the mixed metaphors, ambiguous initials, and bizarre queries make her diary entries as funny as any of Micawber's letters. But she takes a "dreadful luxury" in making the most of Dora's afflictions, and settles at last for a rich, older husband.

So, too, Emma Micawber is as prone to dramatic abuse of language as her husband Wilkins. The letters they send to David and Traddles match perfectly: Both Micawbers have something to say, but nothing more is said by their wordy letters than that they have something to say. Abetting her husband in the delusion something will turn up, sending a child into a pawnshop, weighing with hilarious prudence Mr. Micawber's chances of becoming a judge or the governor of Australia, Mrs. Micawber is just as comic and just as culpable as her husband. While the Micawbers are leaving London, "a mist cleared from her eyes," allowing her to see for a moment how young the abandoned David actually is. But it is only for a moment, and when they next see David, Mrs. Micawber leads the room in a chorus of "Auld Lang Syne."

Comedy is finally no cure for what ails language. For all his bounce and drama, Micawber is not the father David needs and cannot prevent the "waste of promise" Murdstone intends by sending the boy to the city. Dickens presents in *David Copperfield* a London full of falsity and linguistic abuse: spurious names on shop-fronts and warehouses, forgeries, meaningless signatures on bills and I.O.U.s, a gentility so counterfeit even lawyers and schoolmasters pretend to it, the whole commercial world as a systematic perversion of naming. "Nothing's genuine in the place, but the dirt," Betsey declares. "It would be no pleasure to a London tradesman to sell anything which was what he pretended."

And to oppose that falsity and abuse, Micawber has only more falsity and more abuse—delightful falsity and comic abuse, a joy in living no villains ever know, but at last no remedy for the fatherless: Leaving London, Micawber hands the "disbanded" Orfling back to the workhouse and the orphan David off to the carman Tipp. The comic characters may escape destruction, may act happily in their imaginary dramas, may even succeed on the distant stage of an opportune Australia, but they cannot prevent the abuse of names. Micawber has the rhetoric of heroic drama, which makes him comic, boisterous, and fun. But David must look elsewhere for the real order of naming, must make his long trek to Dover to seek true names.

IV

David as he grows is a victim of naming. At each new stage of life, he receives a new name; and each name is a forecast, a symbol, and an example of the way his namer will treat him. But even while he is a victim of his namers, he is actively gaining over naming the mastery that will eventually release him from his namers. Names consistently fascinate the young boy.

"Did you give your son the name of Ham," he asks Dan Peggotty, "because you lived in a sort of ark?" When Emily talks forebodingly of David's parents being gentlefolk while "My uncle Dan is a fisherman," blind David responds, "Dan is Mr. Peggotty, is he?" At Creakle's school, at Omer's shop, at the prison and the warehouse, reference and address always catch David's attention.

And names continue to fascinate him as he grows. Arriving at Betsey's, he shows both his sensitivity to names and his imperfect understanding:

> "I suppose," said my aunt, . . . "you think Mr. Dick a short name? . . . You are not to suppose that he hasn't got a longer . . . Mr. Richard Babley—that's the gentleman's true name."
>
> I was going to suggest, with a modest sense of my youth and the familiarity I had been already guilty of, that I had better give him the full benefit of that name, when my aunt went on to say:
>
> "But don't call him by it, whatever you do. He can't bear his name."

David assumes Annie is the Doctor's daughter, and is surprised to hear her called "Mrs. Strong." At Betsey's house, at Wickfield's office, at Strong's school, David struggles to master the order of names.

He thinks he has mastered that order before he really has. Out on his own for the first time after his adoption, David answers a coachman with an assertion of rank by naming— "'Yes, William,' I said condescendingly (I knew him)"—and is promptly bamboozled into sitting outside the coach. After graduation, "Daisy" David has fall after fall (from his drunken fall down the stairs to his fall in fortune) while seeking his place in the order of names. "We wasn't aware," a waiter apologizes to Steerforth, "as Mr. Copperfield was anyways particular"—meaning they did not suppose David to be particular about his room, but saying David is no one in particular. David is "dreadfully young," but first under Steerforth's tutelage and then under financial necessity, he begins to assert himself. Dickens lets names show the young man's progress in the social order: David plays at calling Peggotty "Mrs. Barkis," only to call her Peggotty thereafter; he dreams of being allowed to call his employer's daughter "Dora"; he priggishly warns

Traddles against "lending his name" to Micawber by co-signing a loan. At the debauch with Steerforth, at Mrs. Waterbrook's "blood" dinner, at the party ruined by Littimer, at the encounters with the Murdstones, at Mrs. Crupp's "guerilla warfare," at the confrontation between Mr. Peggotty and Mrs. Steerforth, David learns the order of names—slowly, but nonetheless firmly and with "earnestness."

And at last, at twenty-one, David is a master of names, a namer of himself and others. "Come legally to man's estate," David is the proper son of his "father-in-law" Murdstone. Become a political reporter, he has "tamed that savage stenographic mystery," and now, like Murdstone, sees through language: "I am quite an Infidel" about parliamentary speeches, he declares. And like Murdstone, he takes a child-wife.

Even without Betsey's nudgings, the parallels between Clara and Dora are obvious: Both are bewitching orphans and incompetent housekeepers, both have two-syllable names ending in -ra, both suffer a husband's desire to reform them, both lose an unnamed child. David's similarity to Murdstone is deepened when we remember Murdstone is left unpunished at the novel's end. Not exactly excused by David's treatment of Dora, much less redeemed, Murdstone is nonetheless beyond David's power to sentence: The man is doubly guilty (as his second marriage proves), but the narrating David cannot impose the penalty—for he himself had tried to turn Julia, Traddles, and even Betsey Trotwood into his own "instruments," his own Misses Murdstone, in the reformation of Dora.

Of course, David is not really Murdstone. He is as much Micawber, and though he wallows in politicians' words, he also begins to spin his own. David and Dora keep house with even more comedy than the Micawbers (who never had the money to treat Emma as a doll or cookery as a game). Humor is Micawber's legacy to David: Clara did the same silly things Dora does, but Murdstone "sitting stern and silent" lacked the grace to laugh.

And yet, just as Micawber offered no cure to Murdstone for David as a child, so he offers no alternative for David as an adult. "I wish to God," Steerforth mourns, "I had a judicious father these last twenty years." Every character of David's generation in *David Copperfield* has lost at least one parent, and this general orphaning deprives them of good models for being adults. When the Micawberish life with Dora wears thin, David sees only the dangerous model of Murdstone to which he can turn.

G.K. Chesterton famously bemoaned the "wrong ending" of *David Copperfield*. But had it ended without Dora's death and David's remarriage, the novel would have marked the triumph of Murdstone—proving that words are empty, that names are merely screens for power and desire, that villains are at least epistemologically if not morally correct. David plays Murdstone badly, because David is basically a good man. But his mastery of names has failed to make him happy, for he has not found the truth to match his morals.

V

Rival epistemologies argue about the transformation of percepts into concepts and concepts into words, and argue about the way in which language reaches back to influence conception and conception reaches back to influence perception. But all epistemologies agree there are no *pure* names, no linguistic gestures that somehow skip over concepts to point straight to things. All speech—even naming—passes through its speaker, and by that passing through, becomes vulnerable to desire. Convention may limit choices for a name (this is the screen of politeness), but it never eliminates choice: In a language as rich as Victorian English, the name chosen for reference or address always reveals something of the namer.

We must speak, however, and when we speak we distinguish things with conceptual distinctions (this is the screen of grammatical necessity). The personal identity and self-knowledge David seeks may be delusions— the over-blessed ending of *David Copperfield* holds little promise of their reality—but seek them he does, and for there to be such things as identity and knowledge, there must be such a thing as *truth*: an intelligible and speakable correspondence between those conceptual distinctions and the distinctions that exist in reality. David must find in names a unity of concept and thing beyond the power of the namer and the impotence of the named. Dickens must put in *David Copperfield* an alternative to Murdstone's grim success and Micawber's cheerful failure.

Hints of this alternative appear throughout the novel in the odd asides about words and language. Just as the lettering on tombstones seems to speak to Pip in *Great Expectations*, so the names carved on school-desks speak to David of the carvers, Clara's indecipherable numerals speak of her housekeeping, and the cabalistic shorthand signs echo the Parliamentary speeches David reports with them. So too sounds speak to certain listeners. "Dora!" David thinks, "What a beautiful name!" "Sophy—pretty name, Copperfield, I always think?" Traddles returns. Warping names to match their bearers, Betsey often hears the sound of names as significant.

And in fact something *is* significant in names. Steerforth charms the Peggottys with his quick grasp of their names. Micawber chants "Heep" as a "magic word." Just as Barkis announces his marriage by saying he should write "Clara Peggotty Barkis" on the cart-tilt, so David feels the "visionary connexion" of names on his marriage license. And so too, the first abuse of Doctors' Commons David denounces is divorce by declaration of wrong name—indeed, he has to go out of his way to denounce this abuse, for the ability to obtain a divorce by claiming one had been married under a false name was eliminated long before David arrives at Doctors' Commons.

But what the significance of names is, the young man has somehow missed before Dora's death, somehow fallen short of grasping in his first try at adulthood. David would imagine as a boy that he was a character from a book: Roderick Random or Tom Jones or Captain Somebody of the Royal Navy who never had his ears boxed by Mr. Murdstone with a Latin Grammar. And "the Captain was a Captain and a hero, in despite of all the grammars of all the languages in the world." But David as he grows loses this childish sense that names might name things as they are—that there is a real significance to names.

Both his Canterbury fathers try to give it back to him. Only Dr. Strong and Mr. Dick are called "philosophers" in *David Copperfield*, and though the title is given humorously, there is in fact something philosophical about their sense of names. "I have sent [the Doctor's] name up, on a scrap of paper, to the kite, along the string, when it has been in the sky, among the larks," Mr. Dick declares, "The kite has been glad to receive it, sir, and the sky has been brighter with it." When young David called the sailor with the ship's name "Skylark" on his chest "Mr. Skylark," he still had this philo-sophical sense, as he did when he first met the Doctor:

> I learned, at second hand, . . . how the Doctor's cogitating man-ner was attributable to his being always engaged in looking out for Greek roots; which, in my innocence and ignorance, I

supposed to be a botanical furor on the Doctor's part, especially as he always looked at the ground when he walked about, until I understood that they were roots of words, with a view to a new Dictionary which he had in contemplation.

David Copperfield is a novel of recollection, as Dickens reminds us in many ways, and all recollection is selective, organizing memory for a present purpose. "It's in vain," Betsey warns, "to recall the past unless it works some influence upon the present." We must take seriously the fact that the narrating David—seeking self-knowledge in recollection—takes an extraordinary interest in words. He remembers in the past tense how the Murdstones robbed him of words and memory, and interrupts his recollections to wonder in the present tense where forgotten words go. Recalling the repeated phrases of Dora's aunts, he remarks, "I had (and have all my life) observed that conventional phrases are a sort of fireworks." Recollecting the male Micawber's thanks to the female Betsey "as between man and man," he comments, "I don't know that Mr. Micawber attached any meaning to this last phrase; I don't know that anyone ever does." Into Micawber's dramatic denunciation of Heep, the narrating David intrudes with a two hundred and forty-three word present-tense complaint about the "piling up of words."

Certainly David pictures himself as born to use words to tell stories. He remembers taking refuge in his father's books and a desperate sort of reading—"reading as if for life." He read then not as a story-reader, but as a story-teller, for he needed to create an "imaginative world" to escape the Murdstones. The power to make words come alive is something he had before the Murdstones came (with the epitaphs in church, the Lazarus story, the Crorkindills book). But looking back at that reading of his father's books (the only legacy Murdstone does not usurp), he sees the moment when he first understood he had this power, and he exploits it for the rest of his life.

There is a moment late in *David Copperfield*, however, when story-telling is no help. David's child is dead and his wife dying. Heep seems certain to marry Agnes, and Traddles unlikely to marry Sophy. Steerforth has thrown off Emily, while the re-encountered Murdstones prove to be beyond David's reach. Betsey is bankrupt and haunted by her nameless husband. Mr. Dick has rescued the Strongs, but only in a way that crystallizes David's worry about his own "undisciplined heart." Ironically, the moment comes just when David has succeeded as a writer. He can throw off parliamentary reporting for fiction; he can support his wife; people recognize his name. But it is to no purpose. David has mastered names and earnestly made his way, but he is not happy.

It is at this moment, however, that David begins to see the alternative he missed in mastering names as screens for power and desire, for it is as at this moment Dora rescues him. When David says he loves her, Dora replies in a telling circumlocution, "Without a story—really?" Settling in his new house, David's old fear of being found out false wells up again, and he feels like an imposter waiting for "the real master" to come home. But life with Dora is not a story, and David's mastery of words is no help for his imposture.

Dora had warned him, however, about true names: "I don't mean, you silly fellow, that you should use the name [Child-Wife] [...] I only mean that you should think of me that way." David's project of reforming Dora must be given up, because Dora is already formed; David's desires are vain, because Dora is already complete. It is "better to be naturally Dora than anything else in the world," he at last decides. Since he cannot adapt Dora to himself, he resolves to adapt himself to Dora.

And yet, through the failure of Wickfield's assumption of "some master motive" in each person, Dickens warns against oversimplification. "Things must shrink very much," Betsey declares, "before they can be measured off in *that* way." David's resolution still seeks, by an act of earnest will, to reshape things to match their concepts. This was the moral practice Betsey claimed to have: a reformation not of others but of herself, a self-shaping by self-naming. As Dora's illness deepens, and "Little Blossom" fades despite Betsey's care, David begins to see even Betsey's earnestness is not enough. When Dora says she was not fit to be a wife, he answers, "Oh, Dora, as fit as I to be a husband!" With Dora's death, David at last gives up trying to form even himself. When he finds Steerforth and Ham "drowndead" together (making the connection of nautical and theological matters that Steerforth had mocked in Doctors' Commons and that had seemed so odd with the sailors in church at Dora's wedding), David at last reaches an adult grasp of names beyond the childish assumption of meaning and the adolescent assumption of emptiness. He sails for the continent and begins his autobiography.

VI

The use Dickens makes of names in *David Copperfield* originates in dialogue, for speech requires relations be shown by what people say, and the power and desire that lurk behind politeness and grammatical necessity are exactly what people do *not* say, are exactly what language hides. Of course, people sometimes say more than they intend. Heep comes closest to speaking aloud of power and desire, for he plays against the gentility the other characters assume. With his "detestable cant of false humility," he has his own strategy to hide the quest for power, and his desire almost breaks through to words. The irony of consoling David for Betsey's ruin nearly betrays Heep into saying power is itself the aim of desire. While describing his upbringing, Heep says what no one else would: "I am very umble to the present moment, Master Copperfield, but I've got a little power!"

Few characters will speak this way within anyone's hearing, however, and first-person narration limits dialogue to what David hears. Early in the novel, Dickens stretches David's hearing by a simulated eavesdropping, exploiting the gap between child and adult: Quinion (discussing the charms of Mrs. Copperfield in front of "Brooks of Sheffield") thinks a boy alone hears, but an adult overhears through memory. Later, Dickens can obtain this effect only by making David blind to signals of coming events. Rosa's excoriation of Emily—the novel's one explicit eavesdropping scene—is heavily rewritten in Dickens's manuscript, but the published form still leaves us uncomfortable with David's passivity. Dickens must in general accept the limitations of first-person narration, and his primary means for indicating his characters' relations must be the terms by which they refer to and address one another—their places in the order of names.

And yet, though his use of naming may have originated simply in the problems presented when a piece of fiction runs primarily on dialogue, Dickens soon finds a deeper purpose. The order of names has caught his attention, and he does more than use it to express rank and sentiment. Dickens shows both the origin of abuse in extrinsic denomination and the power of names to mask that abuse. And he claims at the novel's end both the possibility of intrinsic denomination and the power of true names to speak the unity of concept and thing.

David Copperfield's growth into the writer of *David Copperfield*—the development of the novel's character into the novel's narrator—requires David to grasp the failure of false names before he reaches to the fullness of true names. But he must find in falsity and failure the possibility of truth and reform. Dickens always believed in truth. Beneath the jokes and lies and abused language, there is for Dickens an order of reality that is finally moral and true. No Cheeryble angels descend at the end of *David Copperfield*; no reformed Scrooge or Chuzzlewit promises to fix the broken lives. But truth at last wells up in the novel nonetheless. Agnes is David's true wife, just as Traddles is his true friend. But it is Dora and Steerforth who establish with their deaths the connections David could not make before. Only upon his return from grieving abroad can he see the truth in Agnes and in the life that Traddles has made with Sophy and her sisters. In the novel's concluding "Retrospect," Dickens puts the goal of autobiography: David as an adult, grasping at last true names.

None of David's names at the end of *David Copperfield* are new. The novelty of Sophy's calling Traddles "Tom" is accented by quotation-marks repeatedly in the final two chapters, but David carefully reclaims only his old names: David, Trot, Trotwood, Master Dav'y, even Brooks of Sheffield. His grasp of names has changed, however, since these were given. True names are not destroyed by abuse, but survive to signify the unity of concept and thing. When the re-met Chillip, who delivered him as a baby, says he cannot remember David's name, David replies, "And yet you knew it, long before I knew it myself." David's names each point to a real distinction in the man, and each of David's reclaimings reveals his grasp not just of the corresponding conceptual distinction, but of the truth—the *correspondingness*—of that distinction. When David puts his name up on Traddles's door but refuses to allow practice in the Commons "under cover of my name," we see his maturity.

Only "Doady" and "Daisy"—Dora's and Steerforth's names for David—are left unreclaimed. "I have forgotten this gentleman's name," the grief-mad Mrs. Steerforth mourns in the final chapter. David Copperfield himself has not forgotten it. But he has at last, in Dickens's eyes, outgrown it.

CHAPTER 7 | THOMAS MANN
AND THE GREAT AMBITION

I

The word *modernism* is used for so many different things in so many different contexts that it seems drained of power to be much help, particularly in understanding literature. Perhaps it means that a writer "uses stream of consciousness," in which case Virginia Woolf and James Joyce are modernists, although D.H. Lawrence may not be. Perhaps the word means "uses experimental techniques," in which case Gertrude Stein and André Gide are modernists, although Franz Kafka may not be. Or perhaps the word simply means "doesn't read like the Victorians," in which case Henry James, Joseph Conrad, and Rudyard Kipling are sometimes modernists, while Ford Maddox Ford and Thomas Mann are sometimes not. (Stephen Kern's 2011 study *The Modernist Novel* provides a good introduction to the various reasons novelists have been called modernists.)

Our ability to apply the label becomes even more vexed when we speak of "High Modernism," which in architecture refers to a profound faith in science and technology, and in painting seems to mean something like "work by artists who deliberately make their art obscure so it would seem different from the kitsch of middle-class life." Still, in English poetry we can speak with some intelligible distinction, I think, of High Modernists (T.S. Eliot, Ezra Pound, etc.) on the one hand, and Low Modernists (Vachel Lindsay, Robinson Jeffers, etc.) on the other. And by analogy, we might use the phrase to identify a group of novelists who had enormous ambition for their work.

We have already used artistic ambition as a way of describing the High Victorians who wanted to make their books what we earlier described as possessing the coherence of a symphony: plot, character, and setting joining with diction and voice to move the novel from the sloppiness of Daniel

Defoe's 1719 *Robinson Crusoe* to the tightness of Henry James's 1904 *The Golden Bowl*. And after that first high ambition for the novel came another: the ambition to make the novel itself the answer to the metaphysical crisis of modernity.

Where the Victorian novel, directed most of all at hypocrisy, had wanted in its highest ambition to illustrate the cultural error and point out the personal solution in the redeemed self, the High Modernists wanted the novel itself to be a solution—namely, the sheer narrative fact of the book becoming a mystical thickness restored to the world. Everything was in their purview. The cosmos was their remit. History and psychology, the philosophical disciplines of epistemology and ontology, science and economics, art itself—all these would come together, if they were submitted to a will and talent strong enough, to provide a new thickness of charged meaning to the world.

Sometimes, as with Thomas Mann's *The Magic Mountain* in 1924, the result was acknowledged as a grand success. Sometimes, as with Robert Musil's unfinished *The Man Without Qualities*, published in pieces between 1930 and 1943, the result was acknowledged as a grand failure. (Both these books have as one of their purposes a complete account of why European culture before 1914 had to issue in the First World War. Is it any wonder, given their enormous scope, that the books would not appear till long after the end of the war they set out to explain?) As a line of the novel, we could perhaps trace this High Modernism down to Aleksandr Solzhenitsyn's *The Red Wheel* (1971–1991), although the book, yet another account of the beginning of the First World War, is probably better understood as a Tolstoy-like saga that has some modernist elements. Or even Oscar Hijuelos's *The Mambo Kings Play Songs of Love* (1989), although the book is really more of a Dickens tale that takes advantage of some modernist techniques.

But if we start with the undeniable high-ambition modernist works of Proust's *In Search of Lost Time* (1913–1927) and Joyce's *Ulysses* (1922), the line runs confidently to Mann's *Doctor Faustus* in 1947 and Ralph Ellison's *Invisible Man* in 1952—and then perhaps to Thomas Pynchon's *Gravity's Rainbow* in 1973. Certainly Pynchon had the ambition, the talent, and the energy to undertake a High Modernist novel, but since the themes of *Gravity's Rainbow* are paranoia, incoherence, and the failure of explanation, the book is in many ways our great anti-modernist manifesto: a declaration that the High Modernist project has failed, and the philosophical, historical, and cultural problems of human existence would not yield to the novel, no matter how grandly conceived.

None of these categories of novels has sharp edges; none of these lines of descent is bold and sure. Still, in a broad and loose sense, we can identify a genuine era in the literary history of the novel with the High Victorians' effort to lay bare truth (as instanced, in our last chapter, by Charles Dickens). And we can identify a later era—our own time, in fact—when all grand accounts seem suspect and even ambitious authors suffer from a cultural failure of nerve (as instanced, in our next chapter, by Tom Wolfe). Between them comes the High Modernist work, its great goals clear in Thomas Mann and his *Doctor Faustus*.

There are readers who do not particularly care for *Doctor Faustus*, while I think it a masterwork of Western civilization: deeper and more powerful than anything else by Mann and one of the small handful of great novels after the foundation of High Modernism by Proust and Joyce in the early decades of the twentieth century. Still, what no reader can deny is the book's huge ambition. We have in its pages the attempt to draw together in a cautionary tale a damning account of the secularizing of Europe and the coming of the Second World War. A complete history of Germany and a modern revision of Goethe. A critique of music. A psychologically profound picture of a madman and the story of his naive friend, a decent man unable to do anything meaningful in the world—his goodness issuing in no small reformations of others or even, really, of himself. For that matter, the book aims at explaining both the metaphysical crisis of the West, its great work all done and its artistic forms exhausted, and the reason for the simplistic lure of Nazism.

In one sense, *Doctor Faustus* gives, above all else, a horrifying picture of the heroic artist. What does a genius do when the whole history of classical music is present to his mind all at once, and thereby, except for parody, he is frozen into immobility? Adrian Leverkühn cannot play a chord without thinking that Brahms had preceded him. He cannot play two notes of a melody without hearing Mozart. He has an ambition for music rivaled only by that of Beethoven—the highest of high artists, the man who once claimed that music operates on a higher intellectual plane than philosophy—but, as the Devil himself points out, Leverkühn cannot hear even

Bach without thinking of the possibilities for music that the old composer has found, perfected, and closed off.

And so he makes his fateful decision. His genius issues in a theory of a new musical system (Mann's novelistic use of Arnold Schoenberg's twelve-tone model of atonality—a use with which Schoenberg was not pleased). But even that is not enough for him to create the masterworks, the actual music, at which his genius aims. Much as he must pursue Esmeralda, the prostitute from whom he catches his disease, he must pursue creativity.

In the imagination of a fever dream—or perhaps in truth—Leverkühn meets the Devil and makes a deal, selling his soul for twenty-four years of creativity. And Mephistopheles, who rarely loses such transactions, keeps his word. The composer begins as frozen by intelligence, his complete knowledge of the Western canon. And so the Devil choses the obvious answer. If intelligence immobilizes him, then Leverkühn needs only to become stupid. Infected with the syphilis that will rot his brain, just as Germany is infected by the dynamic stupidity of the Nazis, Leverkühn breaks through his block and begins to compose new and startling works.

Unfortunately but not surprisingly, they are works of darkness and death. They are parodies not just of old music but of *all* music, declaring the failure of everything old, decent, and good. The violence of a satanic will marches through them. Adrian Leverkühn, the heroic figure of genius in one of the great art forms of the West, becomes first an agent of Satan and then a speechless syphilitic, paralyzed and drooling in a sanitarium for ten years after his collapse.

In this drawing together of aesthetics, history, and psychology, Thomas Mann reveals his great ambitions for his own art in *Doctor Faustus*—just as he is engaged, in a very serious sense, in a critique of artistic ambition. But there is an even higher ambition, an even deeper purpose, in the book. Mann expects us to follow the story and thereby learn to escape it. The inevitabilities of history and fallen human nature become less inevitable by our becoming aware of them in all their complexity. In reading the novel, we are ourselves walking the path of self-consciousness, becoming redeemed, at least a little, in the course of coming to a deep self-knowledge.

The past, the resources on which Sir Walter Scott called, had failed in the history of the novel. The honing down to simple truth, the maturing of the self in relation to the world that Dickens demanded, had failed, too, as the culture lost confidence in the sheer existence of an external truth to which the soul is called. And so Thomas Mann takes the next step, seeking with his novel a way to make the novel itself the device for redemption, the novel as a universe-encompassing work of art that transforms the reader. His ambition wasn't just to write a modernist kind of novel. It was to write a modernist kind of gospel.

II

Thomas Mann wanted so much for a solution to be true. However strange the world seemed, however great the crisis of modernity, there *had* to be an answer. The history of high German seriousness—from Kant, Goethe, and Beethoven on—had taught him that the artist is the strong man who hammers out a heroic meaning for this world of weakness and disorder. And that, more than anything else, is what the German novelist wanted to be.

In a sense, he must have known that it wasn't. Mann's stories contain some of the most scathing attacks on the "heroic artist" ever written, from the pretentious and self-satisfied novelist Gustave von Aschenbach in the 1911 novella *Death in Venice* (lured by the beauty of a Polish boy to linger unto death in miasmatic Italy) to the cold, proud, and mad composer Adrian Leverkühn in *Doctor Faustus*.

But this is perhaps our problem with Thomas Mann these days and the explanation for why his reputation as a great, magisterial writer of tra-ditional novels seems to have faded in recent years, for Mann could never leave the question of the artist alone. Art in our time has been raised to such absurd moral heights—and yet simultaneously dropped to such absurd moral depths—that we do not seem to bother much anymore with the sort of ethical questions that made Mann a great and serious novelist, gaving him his great and serious purpose. The fading of Thomas Mann's fiction from our literary view is a fading of artistic *compunction*, a fading of the no-tion that the writer must constantly subject the act of writing to analysis by the scruples of the moral conscience.

When Mann died in Zurich in 1955 at age eighty, few had any doubt that he had written for the ages. In the long working career granted to few writers, he had stood in public view as an acknowledged master for more than fifty years—from the publication of his first major novel, the immensely popular *Buddenbrooks*, in 1901, through *The Magic Mountain* in 1924 and the Nobel Prize that seemed to arrive as its logical tribute five years later. He followed *The Magic Mountain* with the quartet of novels *Joseph and His Brothers* in the 1930s and early 1940s, *Doctor Faustus* in 1948, and on to the *Confessions of Felix Krull, Confidence Man*, a short story expanded into a novel in 1954.

Among general readers, who now can bring to sharp focus a picture of the man? Or recall in sharp detail one of his novels' characters? Mann is too strong a writer to blend easily into the cloud of unread, unregarded Edwardian worthies, but the edges of his memory seem to have blurred. A PBS television production of his most Edwardian novel, *Buddenbrooks* (the story of the decline of a wealthy bourgeois family through several generations), may have revived interest in the novelist in the early 1980s, but even such standard short works as *Death in Venice* or *Tonio Kröger* (a 1903 portrait of the artist as a young man) seem to have fallen off college reading lists, and his lesser known novels—the 1909 *Royal Highness* or 1951 *The Holy Sinner*—have disappeared from easily available editions.

The work almost always named his greatest novel, *The Magic Mountain* tells the story of Hans Castorp, a young German engineer who came on a three-week visit to his cousin at a tuberculosis sanatorium in the mountains and stayed for seven years. Castorp is "a bourgeois, a humanist, and a poet," as the mountain-top seductress Clavdia Chauchat declares: "Germany all rolled into one, just as it should be!" Mann was very much in charge of his fiction, and his deliberate literary compunction ensured that his novels tended to be fables for the social conditions on which he wished to comment. The symbolic meaning of his characters was never far from his mind while he wrote, and he has—and had, even in his own lifetime—the reputation of clinical detachment from his characters.

Mann had in fact a general reputation for detachment from anything but his art. In a pair of extraordinary letters written during the First World War to his brother (the novelist Heinrich Mann, author of *The Blue Angel*) and his publisher, he seems actually to praise—for providing him with a device with which to end *The Magic Mountain*—the war that was slaughtering millions and destroying the same high European culture that he needed to exist for his writing to have purpose. Mann's greatest weakness as a writer was his difficulty in finding plots, and he ruthlessly annexed private events in his family's lives for incidents in his stories and novels— deeply hurting his children, his brother, and his wife's family, for his stature as a public figure in Germany inevitably led to speculation in the press about the originals for his characters.

But he could also be funny. "My books," he once observed, "are full of fun and music, and I am essentially a humorist." *The Magic Mountain* was begun, Mann said in later years, as a sort of comic companion to *Death in Venice*: a short and lightly fictionalized account of a visit he made to a sanitarium and during which a slight flu was diagnosed as tuberculosis requiring an extended and expensive stay. But the novel grew and grew in his hands, taking ten years and seven hundred pages to reach its conclusion in Hans Castorp's departure from the sanitarium to fight in the war. Along the way, it became a book about many things: a young man's initiation into life and love, the scientific pretense of medicine in treating a disease it did not understand, the desperate gaiety of social life in a hospital for the dying, the strange and almost timeless passage of time as experienced by those withdrawn from the real world, and (according to an interpretation of the novel by the American poet Howard Nemerov, singled out for praise by Mann himself) the universal quest for the grail of self-knowledge.

Despite its enormous burdens of serious meaning, however, *The Magic Mountain* both holds together and stays a comedy throughout its fifty-one chapters. Indeed, although Mann resented interpretations of the novel as a satire, the energy of the humor is what unifies *The Magic Mountain* and drives it forward to its serious purpose. John E. Wood's 1996 translation of the novel enlivens what was deadened in the old Helen Lowe-Porter version: the surprising wit and style, the sheer verve and joy in writing with which Mann unfolds his fable of European culture immediately before 1914.

Even the highly symbolic characters, the Jewish-Jesuit reactionary Naphta and the Italian humanist revolutionary Settembrini, seem almost real people. Wood decided wrongly, I believe, to translate the extended French conversation of the famous Walpurgis Night seduction scene, for much of the humor and sexual charge in the encounter with Madame Chauchat over a hard, thin lead pencil depends on the French within the German: *Parler français*, Hans Castorp sighs, *c'est parler sans parler*. But with his general success at capturing the humor of *The Magic Mountain*, Wood gave a new chance at life in English to what may be the last great novel to attempt in a serious way to express the unity of European culture.

Perhaps the clearest way to get at the serious purpose of *The Magic Mountain* is to remember that all great novels take place at the same location: at the intersection of culture and narrative, at "the dark and bloody crossroads" (in Matthew Arnold's phrase) where the battle over culture's self-understanding gets fought out. Born in 1875—to the generation of German writers that included his own brother Heinrich, Franz Kafka, Robert Musil, and Hermann Hesse—Mann faced all the same problems of culture and narrative that drove his contemporaries to make the turn into absurdity, irony, and self-reference. He had "the gifts, but not the naiveté, of a Balzac or a Dickens," Hermann Hesse wrote in a perceptive 1901 review of *Buddenbrooks*. But though *The Magic Mountain* has some Modernist play in its narrator's self-analysis, Mann refused for the most part to become a Modernist in his fiction, and sought instead the old-fashioned power of the artist to speak the moral truth about man and culture.

"Humanism is humiliated or dead," he wrote in the early 1930s; "Consequence: We must establish it again." Thomas Mann represents for us, I think, something of *the last*: the last true believer in high culture, the last heroic humanist, the last great writer to pledge his faith to the traditional novel—if only it be pursued with enough stern perseverance, enough single-minded conviction, enough scrupulous compunction.

And yet, high culture, for all its greatness in Germany, did not prevent the slaughter of the First World War, the decadence of Weimar, and the horror of the Nazis. For a brief period after the Second World War, it was the fashion for American and British pundits to mutter dark generalities about the "German soul" and sketch intellectual genealogies that claimed nearly every historic German artist or thinker as a father of Hitler. Thanks in part to the love many Jewish refugees kept for high German culture, the fashion mercifully passed quickly. (Among the most often accused, Hegel, Wagner, and Nietzsche seem to have recovered, although Heidegger has once again come under the shadow.)

Only in the most attenuated sense did German high culture cause Germany's national sins in the twentieth century, but the fact nonetheless remains that it could not stop them. Mann may represent the last good

German, the last humanistic German, the last high German: "Where I am, there is Germany," he declared upon his arrival in America as a refugee from the Nazis, and although some laughed, many thought it obviously true. But he represents as well the inability of everything that was best in Germany to resist the triumph of everything that was worst.

In a 1996 biography, Donald Prater takes on the difficult task in convincing us both that Mann's mostly forgotten political writings deserve serious attention and that Mann was a closet supporter of leftist causes. Vague predictions of eventual European union and an unfocused wish for a reunited Germany after the Second World War were more common among non-Communist intellectuals than Prater seems to realize, and they reflect no special prescience on Mann's part. During the early years of the Cold War, the elderly novelist undoubtedly said some mildly silly things about "finding a middle ground" between communism and capitalism, but any attempt to find a love of socialism present throughout his intellectual career soon fails.

In his political writings, Mann seems, in fact, that weakest and most delicate of all things: the non-religious *social* conservative, digging in his heels at each new cultural decline and crying, "Enough!"—all the while trying to explain the last decline. Mann had some religious grounding, and Protestantism plays a significant role in *Doctor Faustus* as the novelist tries to express with religious music the world from which Germany fell away. But for the most part, Mann sought in the preservation of high Enlightenment culture the religion he lacked—and as it slipped away, he felt himself, like Germany, more and more adrift. "Germanness is freedom, education, universality, and love—that they don't know this, does not alter it," he had Goethe declare in a fictional dialogue (published in English as *The Beloved Returns*).

His early conservatism, manifesting itself in support for the Kaiser and the 1914 German war effort, gave way in the 1920s to support for the Weimar Republic and caused some comment in the press. After Mann expressed his encouragement for an "immoral" play written by his son, one German newspaper carried the satirical advertisement: "For sale by Thomas Mann, very cheap: a well-preserved conservative philosophy [...] and a father's cane, scarcely used, exchange possible for a Jacobin's cap in good condition." But in truth Mann never ceased to fight for each new status quo as a defense against still worse changes. In one sense, his stand against the Nazis deserves great praise—as a non-Jew he could, like Heidegger, have stood in well with the new movement anxious for the prestige of famous supporters. But in another sense, his rejection of Nazism was almost an inadvertent consequence of his constant rejection of every change in German society.

Even in his fiction, Mann always tended to speak of times past and social worlds long dead. *Felix Krull*—in which a con-man turns out to be (as all con-men must be) a strongly conservative supporter of a stratified society—is a delicious parody, but it is at last a parody of a nineteenth-century European world that had disappeared long before Mann came to write of it. *The Magic Mountain*, the novel that helped explain what led Europe to the First World War, was finished only in 1924. *Buddenbrooks*, *Death in Venice*, and *Tonio Kröger* all have deeply nostalgic resonances. Only in the biblical and Egyptian fantasies of the *Joseph* novels is Mann set free from his desperate desire that things not change. The good, dull narrator of *Doctor Faustus*, writing in Germany at the end of the Second World War , applauds the defeat of the Nazis, but the story he narrates is a story from the past set among two German social worlds—the rural peasants and the urban artists—that the Nazis and the war swept away.

Prater gives a well-written, accessible, and lively account of the novelist's long life as a celebrated writer. He notices the influence of the family history of suicide—two of Mann's sisters, a sister-in-law, and two of his children—while properly refusing to make it a catch-all explanation of Mann's difficult personality. He shows us Mann's private life, the original incidents and personalities Mann turned into fiction, and, best of all, he shows us Mann's fifty years as a public man, a man quoted in the press on every and any topic of passing interest, but maintaining under difficult circumstances the integrity that led him at the peak of his fame to accept exile rather than Nazism. But he shows us as well the self-conscious and melancholy sense of being the last—the last high German, the last Enlightenment figure, the last writer of artistic compunction—with which Mann always lived. His life work, Mann told one biographer, is "nothing more than a rapid recapitulation of the myth of the Western world and its cultural heritage before [...] the final curtain falls."

Although Mann's political judgments were often naive ("The Nazis as a party I hold to be a mischief that will soon pass," he told an interviewer in 1930), his diagnoses of the deep causes of Germany's diseases were often correct, and he fought those diseases heart and soul. As it happens, his cultural fights were always lost, even as he gained personal fame for fighting them. But he never gave up the great ambition to use the art form of the novel itself to create the unity of truth that he demanded—his demand on full display in the extraordinary aspirations of *Doctor Faustus*.

III

In the simplest sense, *Doctor Faustus* tells the story of a great artist, a composer named Adrian Leverkühn. Narrated by his calm, humanistic friend from childhood, the philologist Serenus Zeitblom, the book recounts Leverkühn's rise to genius and fall to madness. As a young man, he voluntarily contracts syphilis from a prostitute, in order to cut himself off from intimacy, allowing himself to focus only on his art—reasoning that love and emotional investment would only interfere with the work he must do.

Nothing good comes of the arrangement. The syphilis destroys his brain, leaving him ruined as a human being by the story's end. And it destroys his art, as well. However brilliant is his invention of a theory of a new musical system, it issues only in actual pieces of music that are dark and genre-ending: "deathworks," to use the American critic Philip Rieff's useful word. Even the brightest of them, the ostensible comedy, is an operatic adaptation of the appropriately named Shakespeare play, *Love's Labour's Lost*. And then Leverkühn produces his *Apocalypse* and, finally, *The Lamentation of Doctor Faustus*, at the presentation of which he collapses into the final mental paralysis of his syphilis.

As Zeitblom's account spans its forty years, slipping disturbingly between the past and the present, it cannot help observing the political and social events unfolding around the two men. Even the moment at which Zeitblom begins his narrative is revealing. The opening pages are set in 1944, and Germany is deep in a war it is fighting, and losing, on three continents. Over the course of their friendship, Adrian Leverkühn moves from student theologian to master composer and down to a syphilitic shell, rendered insane and haunted by regret—just as Germany had moved from a religious past to an obsession with grand endeavors, and down to the mad socio-political regime of the Nazis.

To achieve this equation, Mann saturates the narrative with historical, literary, and biblical allusions—most obviously with the reference of the book's title to Goethe's *Faust*. Within the book itself, Mann makes the connection more rarely than the reader might suspect. A shadowy Mephistopheles figure does appear, and Leverkühn imagines he has made a pact with him, trading his soul for twenty-four years of artistic genius. That makes Leverkühn the Faust figure, of course, but unlike Goethe, Mann presents the choice to make the pact as inevitable, driven less by Leverkühn's personal character than by something intrinsic to his form of the modern German self.

The story is a broken, strangely wandering one, a labyrinthine network of details and characters that the narrator himself decries as being too dense and tangential. But Mann intends his distracting detours, determined to illustrate with his prose the problems he is investigating and seeking to solve. "The section just concluded also swelled much too much for my taste, and it would seem only too advisable for me to ask myself whether the reader's patience is holding out," Zeitblom admits.

> Every word I write here is of searing interest to me, but I must be very much on guard against thinking that that is any guarantee of sympathy on the part of the uninvolved reader! Although I should not forget, either, that I am writing not for the moment, nor for the readers who as yet know nothing at all about Leverkühn [...] but I am preparing this account for a time when conditions for public response will be quite different—and with certainty one can say much more favorable—when the demand for details of this disturbing life, however adeptly or inadeptly presented, will be both less selective and more urgent.

Leverkühn was born of "a stock of better-off craftsmen and farmers," and his childhood was pastoral, his family living on a farmstead called Buchel that "comprised a good eighty acres of fields and meadows, a share in some cooperatively managed woodland, and a very comfortable timberwork house set on a stone foundation. Together, with its barns and stalls it formed an open square in the middle of which stood a massive old linden tree enclosed at its base by a green wooden bench." Leverkühn's parents are hard working and generous, and they welcome Zeitblom when the school-aged Adrian brings his friend to visit.

What Zeitblom sees there, and what he can never forget as he holds on to his increasingly one-sided friendship for Leverkühn, is how *German* it all is. Zeitblom is not fully reliable as a narrator. He is willing to criticize the Germany for its madness: "Never failing public indoctrination has made sure that we are profoundly aware of the crushing consequences, in all their irrevocable horror, of a German defeat, so that we cannot help fearing it more than anything else in the world. And yet there is something that some of us fear—at certain moments that seem criminal even to ourselves, whereas as others fear it quite frankly and permanently—fear more than a German defeat, and that is a German victory." But he cannot bring himself to the parallel criticism of his friend, a German gone mad.

Interestingly, Zeitblom's dislike of the Nazis is born of his love for the old Germany's pastoral and spiritual past. But it is a past that actually belongs to Leverkühn, however much he betrays it. Zeitblom is only allowed to long for it, as when he visits the Leverkühn farm or attends theology classes because his friend does. And just as he knows that Germany does not requite his old-fashioned love, so Zeitblom knows that his devotion to Leverkühn is not fully reciprocated. When they part ways after spending a great deal of their time in college together, Leverkühn is detached and casual. "I could not help accentuating my farewell with the mention of his name—his first name, as was natural for me. He did not mention mine. 'So long,' he said, nothing more—it was an English idiom he had learned [...] and used merely as a kind of ironic quote. [...] He added a jest about the episode of marital life awaiting me, and went his way."

The man who introduces the two young men to serious music is a teacher named Wendell Kretzschmar. Just as Zeitblom never really possessed the old world he defends, so Kretzschmar is a German American, born in Pennsylvania, who has brought his love of European music back home to its origin. Mann describes him as, "Unprepossessing in appearance, a squat man with a round skull [...] and brown eyes whose gaze was now musing, now frisky, but always given to smiling," and Mann makes him a stutterer when nervous or at a loss—a man whose brilliance is hidden by his affliction.

As it happens, he believed his passion alone would ignite the enthusiasm of the public, and he was mistaken. "It was most regrettable that the local public gave him almost no opportunity to prove his theory. For the few of us who sat at his feet on numbered chairs in the yawning void of the old hall, it stood the test perfectly, for he captivated us with things we would never have thought could so hold our attention, and in the end even his dreadful stutter seemed only an intriguingly spellbinding expression of his own zeal."

Kretzschmar spends hours on the question, "Why didn't Beethoven write a third movement for his last piano sonata?" Zeitblum notes that listeners are not particularly plagued by the ostensibly missing movement, but that does not stop Kretzschmar from playing bits and pieces of the two movements on an inferior piano and stopping every now and then to analyze "its psychological content, including descriptions of the circumstances under which it—along with two others had been composed."

Mann indulges a curious mood through all of this. Music arrives in the novel, introduced for the first time, as a psychologically fraught thing. Even to study a musical composition is to ask questions about the state of a composer's mental health, and the higher the seriousness of musical composition—at which Beethoven stands at the pinnacle—the more the fragility of the human psyche is drawn into the work of art.

Before he dedicates himself to music, Leverkühn pursues theology with hints of the same madness of total dedication. Much to the dismay of both Kretzschmar and Zeitblom, Leverkühn decides to study in the austere town of Halle, which Zeitblom describes as having a "theological air" that "did not do him good." In Halle, Zeitblom and Leverkühn encounter the garrulous and theatrical teacher Kumpf. The name, heavy and thudding, fits the bear-like Kumpf, who appears to take up an entire room: "a tall, massive man, with well padded hands, a booming voice, and a lower lip that protruded slightly from so much speaking and tended to spray saliva." He had a "rugged personality," and though Zeitblom enjoyed his theatrics, he "did not love him."

They encounter as well a teacher named Eberhard Schlepfuss, a name that almost hisses off the tongue for "a scrawny man of less than average height [...] who wrapped himself in a black cape fastened with a metal chain at the neck." Like Kumpf, Schlepfuss references Satan, "the Deceiver," often—but where Kumpf's comic nicknames for the devil are "child's play," Schlepfuss "endowed the Destroyer" with a "psychological reality." Schlepfuss argues that Evil is a necessary complement of the holy, and "the Evil One" was "a necessary outpouring and inevitable extension of the holy existence of God Himself; and in like fashion, vice did not consist of itself, but derived its appetite from the defilement of virtue [...] vice consisted of the enjoyment of freedom, the possibility to sin, which was inherent in the very act of creation."

Zeitblom is discomfited by the professor's position on freedom and what it means in relation to faith in God. This is also a clear point where he references the present political climate of Germany and compares it to Schelpfuss's approach. He declares:

> Freedom is a very great thing, the prerequisite of creation that prevented God from shielding us from apostasy. Freedom is the freedom to sin, and piety consists in making no use of freedom out of love for God, Who had granted it. That is how it came out—somewhat tendentious, somewhat malicious, if I was not totally misled. In short it bothered me. I do not like it when someone wants to have it all his way, takes the word right out of his opponent's mouth, twists it, and creates a general confusion of concepts. It is being done at present with the greatest brazenness, and that is the chief cause of my living in seclusion.

Schlepfuss also insists that, for men, women are a movement away from God and toward the freedom of sin: "Sex was her domain, and how could she who was called *femina*—which came half from *fides*, half from *minus* and so meant "lesser faith"—not have stood on intimately wicked footing with the filthy spirits." It is not then outlandish that Leverkühn, when he decides to eschew intimacy and love, seeks out a prostitute by the name of Esmeralda (the name of the gypsy seductress in the *Hunchback of Notre Dame*) and sleeps with her, even knowing that she may carry syphilis. Thus, ironically, the theological town of Halle becomes the place where the terms of the bargain that Leverkühn strikes with the Deceiver are first laid out.

Zeitblom and Leverkühn's spirited philosophical discussions with their fellow students illuminate the prevailing nationalistic attitudes of the generation then coming of age. Mann spends a considerable amount of time exploring "the powerful immaturity" that Leverkühn and his classmates feel are part of the intrinsic German nature—an immaturity that some of the students perceive as not a handicap but a boon, or an ominous and energetic instrument of revolution. "Maybe it's only our history, our having been a little late coming together and forming a shared self awareness," Leverkühn declares, "that beguiles us with some special youthfulness." And his deeply nationalistic (and unsubtly named) classmate Deutschlin answers, "To be young means to be primordial, to have remained close to the wellspring of life, means being able to rise up and shake off the fetters of an outmoded civilization, to dare what others lack the vital courage to do —to plunge back into what is elemental."

After his sojourn as a student, Leverkühn takes up with a character named Schildknapp, a poet, translator, and freelancer of indeterminate profession, who helps Leverkühn with his opera *Love's Labour Lost*. His name means *squire* in German, with an overtone of a ne'er-do-well. Living for pleasure, Schildknapp is a seducer of girls and more than girls. He seduces Leverkühn, not sexually but emotionally: a foreshadowing of the murky Faustian creature who will seduce Leverkühn into the bargain that will be his undoing, as a man. Zeitblom dislikes him, describing the man in a remarkable assessment that reveals the state of Germany, the influences that surround Leverkühn, and the prejudices of the narrator:

> Schildknapp was something of a sponge. But then given his straitened circumstances, why should he not make use of his good looks and social popularity? He got himself invited out a lot, ate his midday meal here and there at houses all over Leipzig, even at the tables of rich Jews, although he had been heard to make anti-Semitic remarks. People who feel they are held back and not given their due, and who at the same time present a distinguished appearance, often seek redress in racist self assertion. The only thing special in his case was that he did not like Germans either, was steeped in their sense of national inferiority, and so explained it all by saying he would rather, or might just as well, associate with Jews. For their part the wives of the Jewish publishers and bankers looked up to him with that profound admiration their race has for German master blood and long legs.

By chapter 19 in the non-linear narrative, Adrian Leverkühn has displayed his musical aptitude to the public and contracted syphilis from the prostitute honest enough to warn him of her illness. When Leverkühn first visits Esmeralda's whorehouse, he does not have sex with her. He returns a second time, prepared to contract the disease, only to find her gone. He hunts for her, and finds her, willfully absorbing her disease.

Between Leverkühn's visits with Esmeralda, between his learning about the syphilis and his decision to become infected, we learn of the first semi-public performance of one of his compositions, *Phosphorescence of the Sea*, which he created under the tutelage of Kretzschmar. Leverkühn dutifully learned the rules of the traditional orchestral tonality and applied it to great success. Or, as Zeitblom notes,

> *Phosphorescence of the Sea*, though sparkling with sound, was a very remarkable example of how an artist can put his best efforts into a task in which he no longer believes and can persist in excelling in an artistic style which to his mind is already hovering on the verge of obsolescence. 'It's the root canal work I have learned to do,' he told me . . . But to be quite frank, this unbelieving masterpiece . . . already bore clandestine traits of parody, of a general attitude of intellectual irony toward art that would so often emerge in an eerie stroke of genius in Leverkühn's later work. Many found this chilling, indeed repulsive and shocking.

Leverkühn's arrogance, his mockery and "intellectual self-consciousness," are on display long before *The Lamentation of Dr. Faustus*. He eschews the past, the artistic obsolescence of German musical composition. He is encumbered by Germany's musical history, and although he has learned from the masters, he will now annihilate them. As Germany sheds its old skin, so shall Leverkühn.

By the time he has his infamous exchange with the Devil, he has met yet another creature who will have a definitive impact on his decline: the seductive violinist Rudi Schwerdtfeger. Leverkühn is deliberately surrounding himself with the stereotypes of the German bourgeoisie: poets, musicians, patrons of the arts, and descendants of a faded nobility such as Schildknapp. Schwerdtfeger, the violinist will be of particular importance because it is through him Leverkühn finally decides he has had enough of this isolation and makes a disastrous attempt to get married. He proposes through his friend, who then ends up seducing the object of Leverkühn's affections.

Still, the core action of the story is precipitation of the conversation and bargain with the Devil. Zeitblom notes that his friend was never tactile or affectionate, but as the years go by he is becoming increasingly less so. Zeitblom assumes it has to with his self-imposed celibacy: "Only a keenly observant friendship like mine could have felt or suspected such a shift in what these things meant, and God forbid that those perceptions might have detracted from my joy in being near Adrian! What was happening inside him could shock me, but never drive me from him. There are people with whom it is not easy to live, but whom it is impossible to leave."

Zeitblom then shares with the reader Leverkühn's "secret manuscript, in my possession since his demise and guarded like a precious, dreadful treasure." Dreadful is a mild description for an account of chatting with Mephistopheles. Zeitblom correctly describes the dialogue as being dominated by the Devil. It is an astonishing exchange because it reads so naturally and matter of fact, perhaps because Leverkühn wholeheartedly believes that he actually talked to the Devil.

At the first moment, the Devil entreats Leverkühn to speak German (he is in Italy at the time and automatically speaks Italian to the stranger who addresses him so familiarly): "Speak only German! Avail yourself of naught but good old fashioned German [...]. At times I understand only German." Even Zeitblom disbelieves the long and detailed dialogue at first, unwilling to believe the darkness in this document originates from his friend. "It is gruesome to think that the cynicism, the mockery, and the humbug likewise comes from his own stricken soul."

Nonetheless, it is in this dialogue that Mann's design of the novel is partially revealed, and much that had previously appeared in the book is represented for the reader in a new, Satanic light. So, for example, Leverkühn and the Devil discuss "homely and humorous German names" and how much the Devil prefers them. Nothing foreign will do. Names distinguish bloodlines, and ethnicity, and desirability. The Devil talks of Leverkühn's disease—the "furtive venereal meningitis" that "goes about its soft, silent work"—in language that echoes with the death of Leverkühn's sweet, angelic nephew, who comes to visit him and dies of meningitis.

Leverkühn becomes angry when they begin to discuss music—for the Devil puts the central metaphysical problem of the high artist in that age: "Certain things are no longer possible. The illusions of emotions as a compositorial work of art, music's self indulgent illusion, has itself become impossible and cannot be maintained." Leverkühn argues that one can play with forms that are no longer common and thereby elevate the forms into new meaning, only to have the Devil answer, "Yes, parody, but so what?"— in Mann's anticipation of the postmodernists who would gleefully give up seriousness.

After the pact is made, Mann takes the reader back to Zeitblom, who is now reflecting on Germany's wars. He goes on to serve briefly in the First World War and anticipates, in his narrative's present time, the invasion of Normandy. Leverkühn finishes *Love's Labour Lost*, which premieres to acclaim. He composes a symphony and his *Gesta Romanorum*, played by marionettes. And he begins to plan a huge work, his *Lamentation of Doctor Faustus*. In 1930, claiming to have completed the score, Leverkühn invites his friends to hear the work—but, instead of playing the music, he tells instead the tale of his pact with the Devil and collapses into the mental paralysis from which he will die a decade later.

The loss of the war and Adrian Leverkühn's death were written on page one. The collapse of Germany and the collapse of the composer were inevitable facts of history and human nature. As inevitable as God's judgment. And only by joining it all together in *Doctor Faustus*, Thomas Mann thinks, can we step outside inevitability enough to find redemption. The novel itself is supposed to be the Paraclete. The reader is supposed to be the hero, the reformed soul, whose outward journey in reading the book is mirrored in reform. In the highest possible ambition for a novel, *Doctor Faustus* is intended as an instrument of individual salvation—or, at least, such as salvation seemed in those dark days.

CHAPTER 8 | TOM WOLFE
AND THE FAILURE OF NERVE

I

At the end of the twentieth and beginning of the twenty-first century, Tom Wolfe was America's greatest living novelist. Kind of. Lord knows, he had the tools. Was there any author who understood the social meaning of clothes, cars, glasses, words—even the way that people sit and stand—better than Wolfe? Was there any reporter who knew how to make a lightning prose zip in and out of characters' minds better than he does? Was there anybody, writer or not, more in love with the "wild, bizarre, unpredictable hog-stomping Baroque country" that is the United States?

Such writers are rare in any generation, and with his 2004 novel, *I Am Charlotte Simmons*, Wolfe produced a satisfying if old-fashioned story of a young person's education and growth. Of course, "old-fashioned" refers here only to the *type* of book Wolfe wrote. In previous *bildungsroman*—from the high level of Goethe's *The Apprenticeship of Wilhelm Meister* (1796) all the way down to something like Owen Johnson's all-American *Stover at Yale* (1912)—you will find neither Tom Wolfe's trademark prose nor the details of oral sex, coed toilets, more oral sex, and occasional class work that he claims to have discovered on America's college campuses. *I Am Charlotte Simmons* takes the theme that romance died the day easy sex was born (a thesis Wolfe chronicled in his 2000 collection of essays, *Hooking Up*) and splays it like a honey-trap across his heroine's path as she travels from an evangelical childhood, isolated in a town called Sparta up in the North Carolina hill country, to an elite education at the fictional Dupont University.

The eponymous Charlotte Simmons may imagine her scholarship to Dupont will show her the life of the mind, but it's the life of the party she soon discovers college is about. She becomes interested in neuropsychology and does well in class—at first. But then she meets Adam, a nerd who writes for a campus paper, together with Jojo, the school's sole Caucasian basketball star, and Hoyt, the preppy fraternity brother and big man on campus.

As in every novel about undergraduates, the adults come off poorly. That's how such books are supposed to work, and the teachers, coaches, administrators, and visiting speakers in *I Am Charlotte Simmons* are all on the make, in one way or another. But Wolfe doesn't let the children off, either. They are at school primarily to be socialized, the author realizes, and their posturings, connivings, seductions, pseudo-adulteries, and struggles for social dominance are all practice for a less-than-promising adulthood.

The plotlines of the self-deceiving Charlotte's three suitors begin to draw together when Hoyt punches out the bodyguard of California's governor. The governor is a rising conservative political star who is on campus to give a speech—and he is, naturally, receiving oral sex from a coed as Hoyt stumbles upon him. Skinny little Adam wants to use the story to make his name as a muckraking journalist, but Adam has his own troubles. His work-study job, tutoring the basketball team, has seduced him into writing a term paper for Jojo, and the news of that cheating is starting to dribble out.

Bringing all this home in the story's conclusion, Wolfe showed that he had solved, for the most part, the plot-construction problems that weakened the endings of his first two novels, *Bonfire of the Vanities* (1987) and *A Man in Full* (1998). With *I Am Charlotte Simmons*, Wolfe produced a solid, well-reported page-turner.

You wouldn't have known it from the reviews. Princeton's Elaine Showalter was a typical example, complaining in the *Chronicle of Higher Education* that Wolfe was a Peeping Tom, cruel to the professors and envious of the students' sex lives. Worse, he didn't understand how *revolutionary* all that sex is—how feminism has set these young women free to discover their sexuality. It may look, to old men like the then-seventy-three-year-old Wolfe, to involve mostly pretty girls socialized into servicing young men on demand, but that's because *I Am Charlotte Simmons* is a "leering" book. It's the author, not his characters, who shows just how "bitchy" and "status-seeking" a person can be.

There was always a strange envy to Tom Wolfe's detractors. And something more than envy—a resentment, an ache, a *fury*: If I could write like that, a small cat snarls inside their heads, I'd...I'd *change* things in this rabid,

111

racist, right-wing world. I'd zola the rich bastards until they burbled for mercy. I'd dickens the corporate polluters until they drowned themselves in their own sick sludge. I'd thackeray, I'd balzac, I'd *dostoyevsky* everyone who doesn't get it—it, the ineffable *it* of political conscience, the mystical rightness that lets a Princeton professor be a revolutionary and, well, a *Princeton* professor at the same time. God—or Charles Darwin, maybe, or some freak of perverse genetics—put a sword in Tom Wolfe's hands, and the oblivious creep won't use it to smite the ungodly. The man doesn't *deserve* his sentences. Prose belongs to us, by divine right and right of conquest. And here comes this white-suited fake dandy, this *reporter*, to set up camp right in the middle of it, like John Ashcroft—or Gary Bauer or, I don't know, Elmer Gantry—buying the prettiest summer house on Martha's Vineyard.

Besides, they complained, he doesn't know what a novel is. And here we get down, if not to the reason for the complaint, then at least to a bone with some meat on it, for Tom Wolfe, in fact, never did know what a novel is. That seems ridiculous to say, of course. With *I Am Charlotte Simmons* in 2004, he produced his third extended piece of fiction, and with *Back to Blood* in 2012, his fourth, each an automatic bestseller and each guaranteed to start a national conversation. What more do you need from a fiction writer? But there's something else a novel wants to do, some place a novel itself wants to go—some aspect a novelist such as Saul Bellow can't help incorporating even in a bad book like his final novel *Ravelstein* (2000), and Tom Wolfe can't quite find even in a good book like *Bonfire of the Vanities*.

Not that *I Am Charlotte Simmons* entirely lacks novelistic touches, although what makes a novel novelistic is hard to say. Well, maybe it's not that hard. Take the moment in Anthony Trollope's *The Prime Minister* (1876) when the social interloper Ferdinand Lopez, finally exposed and disgraced, throws himself in front of a train—"knocked into bloody atoms" at Tenway Junction. And so the man from nowhere disappears back into nothingness. Yes, the irony is a little heavy handed; yes, the completeness of it all, the clicking shut of the box, is a little too satisfactory. But Trollope couldn't help himself. His plot wanted to do this kind of thing, and an author's best bet is simply to get out of the way and let the story go where it's going.

Wolfe understood at least some of this kind of novelistic satisfaction, and *I Am Charlotte Simmons* contains moments of Trollopian completion.

So, for instance, the insufferable frat-boy Hoyt at last gets his comeuppance. Exposed in the school paper and refused the post-graduation job he'd been promised, he moans that he is "f—ked, f—ked, f—ked, and f—ked," which is (how shall we say this delicately?) rather what Hoyt had done to the formerly virginal Charlotte in the book's longest and most awkward scene.

But there's another thing necessary to make a novel—a kind of presence that haunts the text and draws it together at a level deeper than plot. I don't know exactly how to define it, but take the paragraph in the first chapter of Dickens's *David Copperfield*. The caul in which David was born is sold off at a church raffle as an infallible charm against drowning. We can guess that Dickens didn't plan anything with the incident; we have his working notes for the novel, and it just doesn't stand out as anything seriously meant all. Dickens was frantically scribbling to meet his deadlines for the serialized text, and in the wordiness of the irony he loved to indulge, he threw in the scene to fill up a paragraph and make a weak joke about the purchaser, an old lady who died triumphantly undrowned in her bed, although she had never gotten closer to open water than crossing a bridge.

And yet, there it sat, a detail stranded in chapter one, and Dickens, the greatest unconscious novelist of the English language, could feel it somehow, haunting his story. Why is it no surprise that the church at David's wedding, forty chapters later, is inexplicably filled with sailors? Why is it no coincidence that David ends up practicing law in one of those strange English inns of court whose jurisdiction is nautical and ecclesiastical matters? And when, at the novel's climax, David finds the ruined Steerforth "drownded"—*drown dead*—on the beach with his failed rescuer Ham like lost sons of Noah, we feel the deep currents of fiction, pulling the ark of the story out onto a theological sea. It is for this kind of novelistic touch, this kind of completion, that the reader looks in vain while reading Tom Wolfe.

II

Emile Zola was the writer Tom Wolfe recommended as the best model in a widely noted 1989 essay in which he called for America's novelists to leave their prissy, self-absorbed concerns and go out to report on this "wild, bizarre, unpredictable hog-stomping Baroque country of ours." But he mentioned Dickens along the way, and Dickens is the author to whom he is, in fact, the closest—if only because a Wolfe novel is invariably what, as we've noted, Henry James in his Preface to *The Tragic Muse* called books like Dickens's: large loose baggy monsters.

Along the way in that *Harper's* essay calling from a return of American fiction to the broad canvas of the old-fashioned social novel, Wolfe disparaged the nation's contemporary literary authors writers, with their fine and delicate writing-school-trained prose. In part, like his public quarrels with John Updike, the complaint derives from a writer in the Fielding line of external action who cannot bring himself to admire writers in the Richardson line of internal action. Back in the mid-1960s, Wolfe had mocked Updike's "thatchy medieval haircut" and dubbed the *New Yorker* for which Updike wrote a "suburban women's magazine." After his own bestselling novel *The Bonfire of the Vanities*, he issued he issued his *Harper's* "manifesto for the new social novel." In our "weak, pale, tabescent moment," he wrote, there's no one doing what the art form is capable of. We have lots of talented writers, but the "American novel is dying of anorexia" because they won't go out and *report* on anything.

Still, even discounting his preference for the big-shouldered social novel, Wolfe had some cause for his complaint in the era's fiction. Consider, as an archetypal example, Michael Cunningham's novel *The Hours*, which in 1999 won both the Pulitzer prize and the prestigious PEN/Faulkner award, beating out such works as Barbara Kingsolver's almost equally precious *The Poisonwood Bible* and Tom Wolfe's own 742-page monster, *A Man in Full*. Indeed, Wolfe was passed up for every important fiction prize. There was something about his attempts at sprawling social realism that made literary professionals purse their lips in disapproval.

Cunningham first proved how delicately and professionally he could handle even violence in a much-noticed 1988 story in the *New Yorker*, "The White Angel," a chapter from his delicate and professional *A Home at the End of the World*. It's true that in 1995, with *Flesh and Blood*, he attempted a purely popular novel in praise of AIDS activism. But then, with *The Hours*, he scurried back to the literary fold. And the Pulitzer jurors—the novelists Diane Johnson and Oscar Hijuelos and the reviewer Richard Eder—honored the exquisite professionalism of this tiny book about almost nothing. Nothing at all.

The Hours gets its name from Virginia Woolf's working title for her 1925 novel *Mrs. Dalloway*. It consists of three small narratives, told in alternating chapters and conveyed entirely in that dainty continuous-present beloved by the wistful authors of children's books: "Here is Kitty," Cunningham explains. "Here is Kitty's pretty gold wristwatch; here is the quick unraveling of her life."

The first narrative follows the suicidal Virginia Woolf through a day in 1923 England as she struggles to write *Mrs. Dalloway*, suffers an unplanned visit from her sister, and endures her protective husband. The second follows the unconsciously lesbian Laura Brown through a day in 1949 suburban Los Angeles as she struggles to read *Mrs. Dalloway*, suffers the sexual attentions of her husband, and endures the unblinking gaze of her preternaturally aware three-year-old son Richie. And the third follows the consciously lesbian Clarissa Vaughan through a day in 1998 New York as she struggles to arrange a party for her friend Richard, suffers her ceaseless interior monologues, and endures a day's shopping in lower Manhattan.

The "final intersection" of these narratives is (as Princeton professor Michael Wood put it in the *New York Times*) "a thing of such beauty and surprise" that no reviewer should reveal it—except perhaps to say that anyone who didn't guess that Richard will commit suicide à la Virginia Woolf, or that the 1949 Richie has grown up to be the 1998 Richard, really needs to find another pastime besides reading. What were the Pulitzer jurors thinking? A Diane Johnson novel like 1997's *Le Divorce* doesn't read this way. An Oscar Hijuelos story like 1989's *The Mambo Kings Play Songs of Love* really doesn't read this way. A Richard Eder review…well, maybe a Richard Eder review actually does read this way. "The story of Laura's day has the shimmer of a dream," he gushed in the *Los Angeles Times*.

The answer is, of course, that they were thinking how exquisite and professional *The Hours* is. This was the stick John Updike used to beat Tom Wolfe in a 1999 *New Yorker* review that probably cost *A Man in Full* any major literary prize. Producing what "amounts to entertainment, not literature," Wolfe had "failed to be exquisite," Updike pronounced. Even the not entirely exquisite Norman Mailer complained in the *New York Review of Books* about the author's unprofessionalism. The journalist Wolfe never acquired "those novelistic habits that are best learned when we are young" and thus lacks "the most important and noble purpose of a novelist."

Wolfe was, in fact, only partly right to complain about the disappearance of the social novel. He saw in the world of serious American fiction a thousand heirs to John Updike, all possessing a professional prose so finely honed it seemed capable of cutting to the heart of almost anything. And he couldn't understand why they wouldn't use it to carve up anything important. He missed, however, the extent to which a prose creates its own uses, the extent to which a particular style requires a particular sensibility. It's as though our authors have all been forced to absorb something as exquisite as Annie Dillard's *Pilgrim at Tinker Creek*, a book of semi-mystical nature observation that's been mandatory at writers' workshops for years. And once an author's been *annie-dillardated*, the prose gets finer and finer, and the point gets smaller and smaller.

Updike didn't have to pay much penalty for his prose, and even Dillard had interesting things to say. But in Wolfe's mind, their children have all been ruined. They write like angels, of course; indeed, they *are* angels, so disembodied that an infinite number of them can dance on the head of a pin. Even while she's denouncing capitalist America, the Pulitzer runner-up Barbara Kingsolver sounds like an ethereal dove gently expiring from consumption. Alice Munro—whose collection of stories, *The Love of a Good Woman*, won the National Book Critics Circle award that same year—has a prose so fine it can't lift anything heavier than a small cup of tea. There's a description of a china cupboard in her story "Cortes Island" so beautiful and profoundly pointless that it has to be read to be believed.

And Michael Cunningham? When first reached with the news of his Pulitzer, he announced he was going to sit down and "have a good cry." His readers might have guessed as much. In truth, Cunningham's *The Hours* deserves its prizes. Its exquisiteness is measured by such passages as "But there are still the hours, aren't there? One and then another, and you get through that one and then, my god, there's another." And its professionalism is measured by its simultaneous use of all three of the tricks by which our angelic writers cobble up the appearance of a subject on which to shower their perfect prose.

With Virginia Woolf's suicide, Cunningham found the mock gravity of historical tragedy. With his jumbled narrative, he indulged the faux sophistication of a literary puzzle that Michael Ondaatje worked up for *The English Patient*. And with his recasting of *Mrs. Dalloway*, he exploited the literary density that derives from retelling nowadays everything from Dickens's *Great Expectations* to Nabokov's *Lolita*. With all this going for it, who wouldn't pass up Tom Wolfe's *A Man in Full* to give Michael Cunningham's *The Hours* a Pulitzer? The prize novels of America ought to come with a warning label: *The author you are about to read is a professional. Don't try this at home.*

III

Unfortunately, Wolfe's complaint about the failure of one of the streams provided to the art form by the eighteenth-century novelists did not guarantee him success at writing a novel in the other stream. Fielding's triumph with *Tom Jones* in 1749 was not created by *Shamela*, the 1741 book in which Fielding mocked Richardson's *Pamela*. What Wolfe wanted was a big novel of social commentary, attention cast outside the self to reveal the hypocrisies and failures of the culture. He had *ambition* for the novel, in the sense in which we used the word to describe Thomas Mann's work. And if it wasn't ambition at Mann's cosmic level, still Wolfe possessed something that few other writers in his time seemed to have. He wanted the novel to do something in the world. He wanted it to make a difference. He really did want to be Zola or Dickens.

His difficulty is the same metaphysical one we have been pointing out since the first chapter. The moral force of descriptions of hypocrisy and cultural failure depends on the existence of a superior moral frame—a yardstick with which to measure the distance from the ideal—and where shall we look for that today? Even more, Wolfe needs a greater thickness than the world seems to possess. He needs, in fact, that general Protestantism of the Air, as we called it, the background assumption of cultural significance, to carry out his project. And he just can't find it.

What he discovers instead is the culture's failure of nerve, and it ruins the attempt to go where he wants to go. The ending of a Tom Wolfe novel is usually a disaster, or at least a minor fall, because the resources necessary to conclude a story of justification and sanctification simply do not exist for him. He does not see them in the culture, and he does not see them in himself. The novel, we have argued, was born as an eighteenth-century, Protestant-inflected art form to address the problems of a modernity that

117

was itself created when Protestantism joined the other elective affinities that pushed Western civilization out of the Middle Ages. One of the things the novel wants to do is align, through a narrative journey, three disparate elements: the actual body in the world, the self-conscious self in the mind, and the ideal self as a redeemed and sanctified being. But if we lack a Protestantism of the Air, the cultural confidence in the notion that these three might and should come together, then the novel is not an art form that will help us. It's not something that can really tell us the way we live now or, more important, the way we ought to live tomorrow.

IV

I Am Charlotte Simmons is tighter than Wolfe's 1987 *Bonfire of the Vanities*— much tighter than his 1998 *A Man in Full*—but in all his fiction, Tom Wolfe can't help sprawling, more or less the way Dickens does. Dickens will always waste a page describing an inn, if his characters happen to wander into one, and Wolfe will always describe the "alarmingly detailed color photographs of the house specials" in the restaurants his characters chance to enter: "huge plates with slabs of red meat and gigantic patties of ground meat fairly glistening with ooze [...] great molten slices of cheese, veritable lava flows of gravy, every manner of hash brown and french-fried potato, fried onion and fried chicken, including a dish called Sam's Sweet Chickasee, which seemed to consist of an immense patty of skillet-fried ground chicken beneath a mantle of bubbling cream sauce."

But, then, Dickens came to that sprawl through a different path. He learned how to write a novel by reading the loose-jointed picaresques of eighteenth-century English fiction, and onto their extension he forced the thematic depth and symbolic unity that became the definition of the Victorian novel. Wolfe learned instead how to write by producing nonfiction——namely, the series of coruscating essays he collected in *The Kandy-Kolored Tangerine-Flake Streamline Baby* and *The Pump House Gang*, the apotheosis of the 1960s "new journalism."

Those essays had a prose so fast it almost scorched you. "Right this minute, one supposes, he is somewhere there in the innards of those 48 rooms," he wrote in a 1965 piece about visiting Hugh Hefner at the Playboy mansion, "under layers and layers of white wall-to-wall, crimson wall-to-wall, Count Basie-lounge leather, muffled, baffled, swaddled, shrouded, closed in, blacked out, shielded by curtains, drapes, wall-to-wall, blond wood, screens, cords, doors, buzzers, dials, Nubians—he's down in there, the living Hugh Hefner, 150 pounds, like the tender-tympany green heart of an artichoke."

It was a prose straining with voice, more voice than English writing had heard at least since the 1950s, when Dylan Thomas's reminiscences in *A Child's Christmas in Wales* taught a generation of writers just how much could be done with run-on sentences, and maybe since the 1910s, when G.K. Chesterton taught readers just how pointed with paradox the English language could be. In Tom Wolfe's young hands, what counted was speed— a compulsive impulse, an excitement roaring through the essay, refusing to allow the tugged-along reader to realize how many thousands of words were spilling across the page.

Gradually, from his 1968 report on Ken Kesey's LSD adventures in *The Electric Kool-Aid Acid Test* to his 1987 transition to fiction in *The Bonfire of the Vanities*, Wolfe toned down the signature tricks of his early writing: the bouncing sentence fragments, the multiple exclamation points, the nests of ellipses, the spume of interjected half-quotations—*Zowie! Ka-boom! Craaash!* But the prose remained detail-driven and focused on the precise touches that mark social distinctions from his first novel, *The Bonfire of the Vanities*, to the 2012 *Back to Blood*.

And why not? Few other novelists were doing it, and Tom Wolfe proved he was the best social reporter since Thackeray. In the early scene *I Am Charlotte Simmons* in which Charlotte's hick parents meet the wealthy, sophisticated parents of her roommate at freshman orientation, or the scene in which Jojo becomes conscious of the ease with which the black members of his basketball team move and talk, or the scene in which Hoyt and his fraternity brothers discuss their clothes, Wolfe provides details no other writer of his time could even approach.

But those details somehow lack the deeper coherence, the Dickensian imagination, that pulls a baggy monster together. *I Am Charlotte Simmons* has its genuinely novelistic moments, in the sense that we noted in Trollope. There's the intersection of neurology and social reinforcement in the mainstreaming of open sex, for example, signaled in the book's epigraph, a brief description of the work that won a Nobel Prize for a psychologist from Dupont University. And there's the abiding interest in masculinity, a bell rung repeatedly by chapters ending with the word "man." The trouble is that big themes aren't quite enough, any more than Trollopian plot satisfactions are quite enough. All of Wolfe's details, the sharp observations snapped out in lightning prose: They want to do something that Charles Dickens could let them do and Tom Wolfe cannot. They want to cohere, they want to inform one another, they want to *hook up*.

We could do some deep think here about the cultural and linguistic advantages Dickens had in a Victorian world in which you didn't actually have to deflower your heroines on stage; we've clearly lost some shared social intelligence that once helped the novel along, and the level of naiveté—the level of virginity, for that matter—that *I Am Charlotte Simmons* needs in its heroine to build an undergraduate *bildungsroman* probably doesn't exist anymore.

But perhaps the point can be made well enough simply by observing that Tom Wolfe is America's greatest living novelist. Kind of.

V

Perhaps the point can be made even more clearer with his prior book, *A Man in Full*. Even back in the *Esquire* and *New York* magazine essays that made him famous (collected in the two 1960s volumes, *The Kandy-Kolored Tangerine-Flake Streamline Baby* and *The Pump House Gang*) Wolfe had a prose that was novelistic, in a sense—the reader never sure whether the words were coming from the author or his subject.

"This could be so perfect," as Wolfe wrote of a young photographer waiting hour after hour for a celebrity shot. "He, Clancy, will have Natalie Wood all to himself. *Shock*—the real Natalie Wood will be... *his in the dark*. None of those idiots like Penner, with his Leica, what a joke, $400 for a camera when what he needs is a complete brain job—but Penner and none of them are out here and Clancy will have Natalie Wood all to himself, if she will only come out of the hotel."

Such tricks once seemed the very essence of their Day-Glo times: the 1960s in its authentic, energetic, razzle-dazzle voice. But as time went by, they began to seem embarrassing, and Wolfe spent years scrubbing them from his writing. There wasn't much hint of politics in the author's early nonfiction, but one of the first suggestions that he wasn't a standard-issue American liberal came in the 1968 essay "Jousting with Sam and Charlie," a surprisingly sentimental account of American Navy pilots rising at 5:45 each morning to fight in Vietnam—which was also the first essay in which Wolfe began to minimize his verbal tics.

In *The Electric Kool-Aid Acid Test*, his deadpan tale of Ken Kesey's careening across America in a bus filled with a gang of aging hippies known as the Merry Pranksters, it was hard to tell just what Wolfe himself thought of it all. And even in the 1970 *Radical Chic & Mau-Mauing the Flack Catchers*, a devastating portrait of pretension at a New York high-society party for terrorists hosted by Leonard Bernstein, the old voice still remained. But from his 1975 mocking of contemporary art in *The Painted Word* to his 1979 tale of the birth of NASA in *The Right Stuff* and on to his 1981 tirade against modernist architecture in *From Bauhaus to Our House*, our picture of Wolfe came clearer—his goals, his ambitions.

Proof of just how good a writer he was can be found in the fact that, in *A Man in Full*, he eliminated nearly all the tricks—and still what remains is pure speed. "They were clad in the lumpish, padded, metal-gray Zincolon gloves and freezer suits with Dynel fur collars the warehouse issued," he writes about the crew working in the deep-freeze unit of a food wholesaler early in the novel. "On the backs of the jackets was written CROKER in big yellow letters that looked lemony in the fluorescent light. Beneath the freezer suits they wore so many combinations of long johns, shirts, jerseys, sweaters, insulated vests, and sweatsuits, they were puffed up like blimps or the Michelin Tire Man [...]. They were known as the crash'n'burners, and they called the freezer the Suicidal Freezer Unit."

What was called the "New Journalism" was born with Norman Mailer's reports on the 1960 presidential election and the True Crime techniques of Truman Capote developed for *In Cold Blood* in 1966, and it reached some of its wild first-person culmination in Hunter S. Thompson's *Fear and Loathing on the Campaign Trail, 1972*. But the school of reporting may have found its purest expression in Tom Wolfe's writing, for that New Journalism prose always involved techniques that were more novelistic than journalistic: zeroing in on the strange particular lives of individuals who somehow manage in their very particularity to reveal huge swaths of the culture and the times. It was the kind of reporting at which Thackeray had excelled—

the Thackeray whose *Vanity Fair* the title of Wolfe's first novel deliberately echoed. And in fact, *The Bonfire of the Vanities* was the first Thackerayan novel English literature had seen in a long, long time.

Perhaps even more than Thackeray—more than any novelist other than Defoe, Austen, and Trollope—Wolfe knows the importance of money. Just as Sherman McCoy in the wild 1980s financial world of Wolfe's first novel was going broke while making $980,000 a year, so Charlie Croker, an Atlanta real-estate developer, is struggling with millions of dollars of bad debt in the confused 1990s corporate world of Wolfe's second novel.

Charlie, the hero of *A Man in Full*, is an enormous sixty-year-old man: a local boy made more than good, a former football star at Georgia Tech, and a naïf about to be destroyed by the banks that made him enormous loans to build his "Croker Concourse," a huge, tenant-less office building-shopping mall on the edge of Atlanta. He doesn't get much help from his second wife—a young beauty in the hyper-thin, 1990s-style that his discarded first wife describes as leggy hipless "boys with breasts"—and the loan officers of PlannersBanc want to repossess his forty-thousand-acre quail-hunting plantation, his jet airplane, his N.C. Wyeth painting, and all the other toys that make a rich man's life worth living.

But the difference between Charlie Croker and Sherman McCoy—that would-be "Master of the Universe" who proved a weakling and a failure (until the awkward ending tacked-on to *The Bonfire of the Vanities*)—is that Wolfe intends Charlie to be a *man*. If there stands a genuine, Victorian-novel sort of theme in *A Man is Full*—the kind of philosophical and literary point on which the High Victorian novel insisted—it's the exploration of what it means to be masculine. Charlie has real courage, enough physical courage to snatch up in his hand a rattlesnake on his plantation, and enough emotional courage as well to stand up to the bank auditors who, in the opening chapter's marvelously captured parody of manliness, try to break the will of their deadbeat victim. Unlike the Wall Street brokers trading derivatives and futures of products they had no hand in producing, Charlie has actually built things, developed things, and left behind something with his name on it, which is both what makes his financial collapse so awful and gives him the possibility to rise above it.

It's a flaw that Wolfe's female characters in *A Man in Full* are blank to the point of non-existence. But their blankness does allow the author to point almost every important figure in the novel toward the question of what it means to be *manly*—in all the old-fashioned senses of the word: how to avoid showing the flinch of cowards, how to hide the emotion revealed by women, how to accept the responsibility refused by boys.

There's the craven loan officer from PlannersBanc with the Dickensian name of Raymond Peepgas. He's going bankrupt on a salary of $130,000 a year, he's borrowed to the limit on nineteen of his twenty-two credit cards, and he owes thousands of dollars in paternity payments to his Finnish mistress, but he has finally decided to do what he thinks is the manly thing and take his future in his own hands—by trying to steal Charlie's financially strapped real-estate empire.

There's Fareek Fanon, a modern, black Georgia Tech football star who may or may not have raped the white socialite daughter of a prominent Atlanta businessman—and the novel's plot thickens as the girl's father pressures Charlie to denounce the accused football player and the city's leaders pressure Charlie to support him.

And then there are the blacks who run the politics of Atlanta. Roger White II, nicknamed "Roger Too White," is a black lawyer who dresses in tailored suits and tries to hide his taste for classic architecture and classical music. The mayor, Wesley Dobbs, is a man wise in the political manipulation of his opponents, and he's trying to downplay the fact that he—like most of the city's black elite—is a graduate of Atlanta's distinguished Morehouse College .

Finally there's Conrad Hensley, a young Californian saving to buy a condo. Conrad's parents were solid, all-American hippies who never bothered to give their son a good education or a stable home. But somewhere along the line, all on his own, Conrad picked up the idea of responsibility. Still in his early twenties, he drives a dented old Hyundai (every character in the novel is closely matched with a minutely described automobile—as though, in Tom Wolfe's world, if four wheels don't make the man, they at least help define him). And he works hour after frigid hour hauling eighty-pound crates around in the Suicidal Freezer Unit of a California food warehouse owned by Charlie Croker far off in Atlanta. But Conrad has to do it—because he's got a family, a wife and two children, and he's got a *duty* that no one else around him seems to understand.

Unfortunately, Conrad loses his job in one of the cutbacks by which

Charlie tries to save his crumbling empire. And then, in a single freak incident, he loses his temper as well—ending up in prison for attacking the tow-truck driver who impounded his car. Though the novel has received considerable attention for its ruthless exposure of the low life that passes for high society down in Georgia, the scenes of Conrad's stay in prison—like the bankers' "workout" of Charlie and the account of the California freezer unit—are the real masterpieces of description in the novel.

What Conrad discovers in prison is the extent to which all men, everywhere, are engaged in contests of masculinity. Violence and honor, prestige and duty, friendship and even physical survival all derive from it—mostly, in the modern world, in mistaken, foolish, and self-defeating ways. But Conrad seems to have a deep, intuitive source of manhood somewhere inside him, and when by accident he begins in prison to read the *Enchiridion* of Epictetus and other works by the ancient Stoic philosophers, he learns at last a vocabulary with which to express and affirm the things he has always somehow known.

It's a little pointless to complain of Victorian novels (as Mark Twain once did) that they often rely for their effects on strained coincidences and unlikely occurrences—that Thackeray wasn't above forcing Becky Sharpe to bump into the one person in London she wants to avoid, that Dickens wasn't above eliminating a particularly nasty character by means of spontaneous combustion. Tom Wolfe was attempting a good Victorian novel in *A Man in Full*, and it is similarly pointless to complain about the plot twists he needs to make it run. So what if it takes an earthquake to help Conrad escape from prison? So what if his California Okie acquaintances from the Suicidal Freezer Unit just happen to know the last remnants of the South Vietnamese freedom fighters in the United States, and they just happen to be willing to provide Conrad with a new identity and bundle him across the country to Atlanta? So what if Charlie Croker's old football-injured knee starts acting up and he needs to hire a male nurse—which is, of course, the profession the fugitive Conrad has taken up?

It is not pointless, however, to complain about the Stoicism that Conrad has learned and that he teaches to Charlie. It's hard to see what genuine use *could* be made of that philosophy Wolfe throws away in a silly parody of Christian revivalism and a preaching of "the cult of Zeus" in the last ten pages of the novel. But even taken at its most promising, Stoicism simply isn't the answer to the problems the author has set himself in *A Man in Full*.

It sounds absurd to say that what the man lacks is culture. With a Ph.D. in American Studies from Yale and his "New Journalism" travels among the glitterati, Wolfe has a much better education than Charlotte Brontë or Dickens or Trollope possessed and a much greater acquaintance with high society than Thackeray had. And yet, somehow, the great Victorian novelists had a culture around them that taught them the things they needed to know. Wolfe knows that a novel wants finally to redeem its hero, but he doesn't seem to know that Stoicism of Epictetus and Seneca and Marcus Aurelius stands in the later years of the ancient world as the great *anti-redemptive* alternative for opponents of Christianity.

Stoicism is at last a philosophy of quietism and acceptance, and the novel as an art form wants to make things happen. Even the stoically inclined George Eliot could have predicted from the first few chapters of *A Man in Full* that Wolfe—no matter how marvelously fast his prose and how telling his social descriptions—was painting himself into a corner. The novel ends with a weak and unsatisfying ending, a jarring retreat into ironic authorial distance, for the simple reason that there is in fact no way to finish off the project the author has begun. What he requires is a vision of how to live the good life, and what he has with Stoicism is only a vision of how to make the most of the not-so-good life.

CHAPTER 9 | POPULAR FICTIONS

I

We have hardly touched the greater part of fiction—the hundreds of thousand of novels produced in the modern world since Cervantes began the flood and the eighteenth-century English writers dug the riverbeds down which the streams of the novel would flow. In a sense, that may be all right. No one can read everything; the corpus of merely the English-language novel long ago passed the capacity of even a lifetime reader to absorb. For that matter, the vast majority of writers, like the vast majority of non-writers, are not particularly concerned with discovering the highest purposes and outermost limits of their arts. Too busy, too self-contained, too humble, or too caught up in the sheer human getting-on with life, they are as the history of the novel rather suggests most of us are: both unique self-directed souls, in themselves, and merely flotsam swept back and forth by the historical tides of culture, as they exist in the social world.

In other words, the majority of novels are not *Waverley*, *David Copperfield*, *Doctor Faustus*, or *A Man in Full*, the books we have looked at in some depth—or, for that matter, *The Brothers Karamazov* (1880), *Tess of the D'Urbervilles* (1891), *Finnegans Wake* (1939), *One Hundred Years of Solitude* (1967), and many others: vital books we have not even mentioned thus far. The everyday novels are sometimes *like* those books, following in their wake and thereby often being wonderful examples of the fiction of their time, place, and kind. But they flood no banks and carve no new channels. They just float along with the established flow.

I have always had a soft spot for books as different as Marie Corelli's truly peculiar and self-obsessed authorial-wish-fulfillment story, *The Sorrows of Satan* (1895), James Hilton's autumnal *Random Harvest* (1941), and Paul Gallico's saccharine *Flowers for Mrs. Harris* (1958), without ever being tempted to do deep readings of them or propose them for iconic status. (Although, like the underrated adventure-story writer John Buchan—whose

1926 novel *The Dancing Floor* is almost like something René Girard might have come up with in its reading of the mythologies in *The Golden Bough*— Hilton probably deserves further attention: a writer whose bestselling success, with *Lost Horizon* and *Goodbye, Mr. Chips*, may have ended up curiously hiding his talent.)

Even liking these books, however, we do not typically feel much desire to provide for any one of them a deep reading of literary theory. In their bulk, however, classes of everyday novels sometimes reveal interesting things about the condition of the art and thereby the condition of the culture producing that art.

Take, for example, one type of novel: the popular novel with some literary pretentions, whether it be of the middlebrow, or the lower-middlebrow, or however one wants to carve up the forehead. The type has always flourished (John Irving's 1978 *The World According to Garp* might be a good example), but in recent decades it seems to have gone into some decline, as the kind of talented writers who once produced it begin to shift their energy to genre novels.

One gain is a rise in the tone of genre work. With *The Plot Against America* in 2004, Philip Roth, always understood as a significant American writer, entered the genre of alternate-history (mostly a subgenre of science-fiction). Thomas Pynchon is another one of many acclaimed writers who have turned, ironically or not, to play with the conventions of thrillers and mysteries.

Meanwhile, John le Carré is routinely named as someone who turned the Cold War spy thriller into art with his 1960s and 1970s books. Patrick O'Brian, with his Aubrey–Maturin series through the 1990s, produced interesting writing in the genre of Napoleonic War sea novels that had been resting pretty much where C.S. Forester's Hornblower stories had left it in the 1940s. For that matter, the Western moved far beyond where Owen Wister, Zane Gray, and Louis L'Amour set it down; very interesting things occurred in the years after Thomas Berger's *Little Big Man* (1964) and Charles Portis's *True Grit* (1968) changed the genre—as witness works as novelistically serious as Ron Hansen's *Desperadoes* (1979) and *The Assassination of Jesse James by the Coward Robert Ford* (1983), and Cormac McCarthy's *Blood Meridian* (1985). The late Victorian and Edwardian writers were very good, with many of the popular novelistic genres invented in their eras, but now is the time to live if you love to read these styles of book.

The turn to genre fiction by talented writers, however, may also show something of what we have lost—offering at least another small piece of evidence that, as we noted in the chapter on Tom Wolfe, the novel has lost a great deal of its nerve. The rise of children's books offers a similar data point. For all the wonderful work going on in that species of fiction, it argues something a little sad about the art form. If to put great clashes of good and evil without irony, if to use the ideas of virtue and vice with serious intent, if to show the world-changing journey as instancing a soul-changing transformation, we have to go to books aimed at the young, then the novel as an art form has given up on a great deal that was once thought its fundamental purpose.

We might see something similar in the exhaustion of certain types of novels—the academic novel, for instance, which was once a lively and new-seeming form but now feels as though it is mostly just going through the motions, a dull treadmill of convention. In part because of pressure from publishers over the last few decades, writers are pushed to produce books in narrowly defined genres, species, and types. It ought not to be all that much of a surprise that these categories get worn out. Still, in their wearing out, we might see more cause to worry about the decline of the novel and the decline of the cultural confidence necessary to produce it.

But let's spend a little more time with certain genres—the graphic novel, for example. And children's books. And the curious history of the middlebrow story.

II

In November 1988, the novel as an art-form sputtered out and died. And a man named Neil Gaiman killed it. None of that is true, of course. At least, none of it is true in the sense of the actual particulars, the genuine facts on the ground.

Novels didn't cease to be written. Novelists didn't forget that book-length fiction was one of the central devices by which modern times tried to explain itself to itself. Publishers didn't fold up their businesses and steal away into the night. There's a lot of ruin in an art-form, and the novel would long continue to gaze out on the world of art it once seemed to dominate. Still, at the end of 1988, a twenty-eight-year-old Englishman began to publish a comic-book series called *The Sandman*, and that publication meant something—something about the fading conviction that traditional fiction was the highest path, the greatest art.

Even the most powerful cultural commitments to an art-form can change, of course. Take television, for example. Through the second half of the twentieth century, it was common to hear nattering about how movies and even "the vast wasteland" of television (as Newton Minnow famously described it) were seizing territory that books once occupied. Marshall McLuhan had told us the medium is the message in 1964. And Neil Postman added in 1985 that television is like Aldous Huxley's *Brave New World* come to life, as we amuse ourselves to death.

But in the late 1990s and early 2000s, something seemed to change in the way critics treated TV shows. The new economics of the internet no doubt was partly the cause, and the resulting capacity to binge—watching many episodes in a row—allowed television programs to indulge (and viewers to appreciate) new forms of narrative arc, new unities of incidental details, and new types of characters. *The Simpsons* (beginning in 1989), *Seinfeld* (1989), and *The X-Files* (1993) seemed very fresh at the time, but they were in certain ways still following (and advancing from) traditional television forms—*The Simpsons* in the line of *The Flintstones* (1960), *Seinfeld* in the line of Jackie Gleason's *The Honeymooners* (1955), and *The X-Files* in the line of *Kolchak: The Night Stalker* (1974). David Lynch's theatrical and cinemagraphic series *Twin Peaks* felt at the time as a breakthrough when it began running in 1990, but ABC, the network airing it, forced changes that weakened the program—in the name of making it more like traditional television.

Less than a decade later, a show such as *The Sopranos* (1999) was under no such pressure. And several programs over the next ten years loudly proclaimed a new reality—an artistic reality in which television had come to believe itself a major art form. *The Wire* (2002), *Lost* (2004), *Mad Men* (2007), *Breaking Bad* (2008), and more besides. These programs formed the new art that felt it had passed what we called above the Cocktail Party Test. They were increasingly necessary to watch if one wanted to have shared conversation about the culture's central art at a party.

Now, consider comic books in a parallel way. Given the status of comic books through, say, the early 1960s, no would have predicted their triumph, much less their repackaging as "graphic novels." In the late 1940s, comic books were an astonishing success, selling over 80 million copies a week, in genres from comedy to horror, superheroes to romance. A decade later, their sales had collapsed, and the genre appeared as much a literary backwater as the long-lost penny dreadfuls, the cheap sensational fiction of the late nineteenth century.

A common way to tell the story is to blame Fredric Wertham, the psychologist whose bestselling book, *Seduction of the Innocent* (1954), became the central text for a brief moral panic in America about the pernicious effect of comic books. But the truth is that the decline of comic books was over-determined. The genre was weaker than its sales seemed to indicate. Television was posed to steal away its fans, while the seriousness of the middlebrow novels of the 1950s kept the genre firmly perceived as lowbrow and embarrassing fare. And, of course, parents and preachers found the worst excesses of comic books easy examples to use in an argument about moral decline.

Stan Lee—the almost mythical figure behind the rise of Marvel Comics from the 1960s on—occupies roughly the morphological space of P.T. Barnum, the man without whom the modern circus would not have come to exist. Or so, at least, the popular-culture critic Jonathan V. Last has recently argued. Stan Lee hardly invented comic-book art, and he certainly wasn't its greatest practitioner. But he created the comic-book industry in its modern form, and without Lee's promotional work, we wouldn't have the twenty-first century's now apparently endless production of superhero movies and cultural references.

As it happens, Neal Gaiman published *The Sandman* with DC Comics, the major rival of Stan Lee's Marvel Comics. The 1980s saw much pushing at the seams of traditional comic-book settings. Frank Miller's breakthrough came with *Ronin* in 1983. Alan Moore produced *V for Vendetta* between 1982 and 1985. But Miller and Moore were, in essence, pathbreaking comic-book writers. Neil Gaiman was something else—a writer with novelistic talent and novelistic goals, writing a comic book instead of a novel.

Some of the reason was surely happenstance. Through his early twenties, Gaiman was mostly just a young writer on the make. He wrote a quickie biography of the pop band Duran Duran. He compiled *Don't Panic*, the "official companion" to *The Hitchhiker's Guide to the Galaxy*. He poured out articles for British magazines under a variety of pseudonyms. And then, through the efforts of Karen Berger, a DC Comics editor, he produced the storyline for comics that revived and reinvented a defunct DC Comics character named the Sandman. The first series would be published in book form as *Preludes and Nocturnes* in 1989, and more than ten other volumes followed—with *Endless Nights* becoming the first graphic novel to appear on the *New York Times* hardcover bestseller list.

Gaiman began to project, he explained in the thirtieth-anniversary edition, with a picture in his mind, an image of "a man, young, pale and naked, imprisoned in a tiny cell, waiting until his captors passed away, willing to wait until the room he was in crumbled to dust." *Preludes and Nocturnes* collects the first series of eight issues of the *Sandman* comic, telling how Aleister Crowley-like occultists capture and contain for decades a strange supernatural being named Dream. Or Morpheus. Or the Prince of Stories. Or the Sandman.

In the original DC Comics version, the Sandman was a fairly standard superhero, albeit one with the ability to induce sleep and influence dreams. In Gaiman's hands, the Sandman became instead an anthropomorphic representation of an eternal theme: less like Superman and more like Death. The strangeness of the times in which Gaiman wrote, the 1980s woes of the modern age, are implicitly ascribed to the absence of Dream, prince of stories—held for a generation while the occultists tried to figure out how to harness his power.

Soon after the story opens, however, Dream escapes and begins his efforts to gather again the tools he had used to perform his work. He travels to Hell to claim from one of Lucifer's demons his missing helm, and he teams up with another DC Comics character, *Hellblazer's* John Constantine, to find his satchel of sand.

The final tool, a ruby talisman, falls into the hands of the insane "Dee," the mad persona of the super-criminal Doctor Destiny. "24 Hours," the portion of the story where Dee uses the ruby to torture people in a diner, Gaiman himself describes as "one of the very few genuinely horrific tales" he has ever written. In the final section, Sandman accompanies his sister—

the grim reaper, another of the anthropomorphic eternals—on an afternoon of her rounds.

In some ways, the *Sandman* books are a disastrous hodgepodge. Cain and Abel are recurring characters. So is G.K. Chesterton. African tribesmen wander in to the book to tell stories. So do punk rockers. It's as though, in this first opening of his imagination, Gaiman twisted the spigot too far, and more came pouring out than comic-book pages could contain.

Through it all, however, he was seeking something akin to the Jungian archetypes. He wanted to reach down into the deep stuff of legend and make his own story out of the root elements of storytelling. Superhero comics always splashed happily in the shallows of myth. Gaiman's *Sandman* tried instead to dive into the deep waters of the mythopoeic.

He would reach his goal better in his actual prose novel *American Gods*. And in the film script he reworked into the story *Neverwhere*. Even such children's books as *Coraline*, such romances as *Stardust*, and such nonfiction as his book on Norse mythology. But some of the novelistic goals he had were channeled away from the novelistic talent he had by their original appearance in comic books.

In other words, the novel as an art-form didn't seem the only place— the obvious, the necessary, the deepest location—for the artistic ambition of the literary genius possessed by Neil Gaiman. And that says something, doesn't it? Something about the fading conviction that traditional fiction is the highest path, the greatest art?

Even in their self-elevated form as graphic novels, illustrated comic books almost always strive for the mythopoeic—which means the fiction tends toward what we previously described as *chanson de geste* texts: stock characters and fixed social types that perform iconic actions. (And thus they differ from the *roman* tradition, the central stream of the modern novel, in which characters are generally required to be more realistic, with individual interior lives.)

Sometimes, in *chanson de geste* texts, the mythopoeic figures may appear as fairly pure Jungian archetypes: the earth mother and the sex goddess, the wise old grandfather, the trickster. They can sort themselves out into types recognizable as Commedia dell'Arte characters: Harlequin, Pantalone, Colombina, Zanni. They can echo old theogonies, from Hindu to

Norse. And in the hands of someone like Gaiman, they can even show some awareness of interior lives.

But for the most part, the modern comic-book forms of *chanson de geste* fiction have streamlined its character types, sanding down the classic figures of Ancient Greek dramas and situating everyone from Aquaman to Iron Man on a moral plane defined by four cardinal directions, like a compass rose:

The Hero—who does the right thing for the right reasons.
The Anti-Hero—who does the right thing for the wrong reasons.
The Tragic Hero—who does the wrong thing for the right reasons.
The Villain—who does the wrong thing for the wrong reasons.

On the moral plane, these characters can blend or even change their identity for any given instance. Superman, for example, is the Hero, but a particular story can have him make a mistake, blending with the Tragic Hero. Batman is the Anti-Hero, doing the good of fighting crime for twisted and vengeful reasons welling up from his childhood traumas, but any one Batman story can briefly morph his character type into the Hero or even the Villain.

In the hands of someone, like Gaiman, with real literary skill, the types are always blended, and often reach into the strangeness—the unstreamlined narratives—of premodern mythologies. But Gaiman's work, from *The Sandman* stories on, are still *chanson de geste* texts. And the question is why a literary artist in 1988 would turn away from realism of the *roman* tradition and toward more mythopoetic forms.

The answer, surely, is the one we have been thinking about all along: the decline of the major forms of novel as devices that, in a cultural agreement between authors and readers, could address the problems of the psyche in the modern world. But the general answer takes a specific form when the impulse is to turn to comic-books novels.

Some hunger is clearly being fed by the graphic novel that the traditional novel felt insufficient to do. Something deep and metaphysical is desired, whether we call successes or failures as art such work as Alan Moore's *V for Vendetta* (1982), *Watchmen* (1986), and *League of Extraordinary Gentlemen* (1999). Frank Miller's *The Dark Knight Returns* (1986) and *Sin City*

(1991). Art Spiegelman's *Maus* (1980). Chris Ware's *Jimmy Corrigan* (2000). And many more—to say nothing of what the novelist Michael Chabon was after when he paid homage to the early generation of Marvel and DC Comics creators in his novel, *The Amazing Adventures of Kavalier & Clay* (2000).

The possibility of moral judgment, the clear sense of right and wrong, is surely part of it. But even more, the comic books possessed a metaphysical clarity about good and evil. It could be as unsophisticated as Captain America's unbearably bombastic adventures against the Nazis after he was created in 1941. It could be as complex as Neil Gaiman's Sandman. But always the modern comic books strove for a clean world. A setting of reality in which heroes and villains are real and do as they must.

G.K. Chesterton once quipped, "Fairy tales do not tell children the dragons exist. Children already know that dragons exist. Fairy tales tell children the dragons can be killed." In the same way, the defeat of evil monsters in comic books testifies to a universe that has moral order and teaches that evil can be overcome. And somewhere along the line, the art-form of the novel found itself too thin, too metaphysically barren, to make any similar claim.

III

We might think, in a parallel way, about children's books. Why is it that so many talented writers have turned to writing in the genre? Even while the novel as a high literary art-form has faded in popular estimation, we have been living for the past twenty-five years in what seems undeniably a golden age of books for children.

Of course, defining what makes a book appropriate for children is difficult. Sometimes a book is in the canon of children's literature just because the writing is so good. Kenneth Grahame's *Wind in the Willows*, for instance, stands as the perfection of its kind: a prose of greeny gold, summer recollected in autumn's light. Rudyard Kipling, too, has the perfect sort of prose for what he does. From *Kim* to *The Just So Stories* to *The Jungle Books*, he paints the strange new world of India in strange new Indian words—none of them quite defined, but all of them given exactly enough context that the child reader can feel the satisfaction of puzzling them out.

Then, too, certain books are remembered simply because they have an ideal premise. When William Golding won the Nobel Prize in 1983, it was mostly for the power of his 1954 novel *Lord of the Flies*. And there's a reason that he based the book on (and made a horror story out of) R.M. Ballantyne's 1857 feel-good children's classic, *The Coral Island*. Ballantyne couldn't write his way out of a paper bag, but *The Coral Island* reaches up to something like the platonic form of childhood's daydreams, in its setting of boys alone on a desert island: a Robinsonade of children without adults.

For that matter, think of Frances Hodgson Burnett, an author with a sensibility so delicate (and a father-fixation so indelicate) that any rational child would smash a window after reading her, desperate for air. But Burnett's 1905 *A Little Princess* nonetheless succeeds as a story, because it provides a room where its natural readers' fantasies can dwell, as the heroine—a little girl, bookish and mistreated—turns out to be the long-lost heir of a large fortune and the ward of an older man who pampers and, ah, yes, *understands* her.

Meanwhile, sheer liveliness of invention can make a book a classic, one set-piece tripping so rapidly on the heels of another that you don't bother noticing how good or bad the connecting story actually is: *Around the World in 80 Days*, for instance, and *The Peterkin Papers*; *Black Beauty* and *The Adventures of Tom Sawyer*, too, different as they are. Good illustrations, as well, sometimes push a book into the canon. I've always thought *Babar the Elephant* was raised above its station by Jean de Brunhoff's drawings, but the *Little Bear* books may be the prime example. Else Minarik's words are no more than passable place-holders for the young Maurice Sendak's art.

Other books stay in mind because, in an inexplicable way, they seem to capture the inexplicability that every child encounters—the unmanageable, and the frantic, and the just plain peculiar. Antoine de Saint Exupery's oddly paced *The Little Prince*, for example, and Charles Kingsley's strange Victorian tale of *The Water Babies*, and much by Roald Dahl. It may not be possible to see Beatrix Potter with a fresh eye (nobody actually reads her; we all somehow only reread her). But, when you get a chance, take another look at the prose and drawings in *The Tale of Two Bad Mice*, one of the weirdest things ever allowed into print.

Still, a number of books are in the received lists of children's classics for the sole reason, as near as I can tell, that they always have been in such received lists of children's classics. What makes Aesop's *Fables* a standard volume for children? Or the far too grown-up *Three Musketeers?* Or the knock-off that is *The Swiss Family Robinson?* Or the inferior horse story *My Friend Flicka?* Or that sick-making tale of the Glad Girl, *Pollyanna?* Or the stale *Little Women*, a book well known mostly because it's already well known?

But as soon as I say that, I realize I may be wrong about Louisa May Alcott. I've always thought the authorial wish-fulfillment at the end of *Little Women* a little creepy, as Alcott invents an idealized husband for the idealized self that is her heroine Jo. Besides, the book is badly paced, falls apart in the second half (setting up the weakness of its sequels in *Little Men* and *Jo's Boys*), and generally ranks below Charlotte Yonge's 1856 *The Daisy Chain* in the genre of stories about the moral and spiritual formation of Victorian girls. But readers I respect admire *Little Women*, and, regardless, the point remains. There is a success that comes only with success; we know these books because we know them, and however well or badly written, their *sharedness* has become their most important quality. That's not at all a bad thing. It is, in its way, a definition of culture: the received stories, the common knowledge, the shared references.

Surely this accounts for some of the phenomenon of J.K. Rowling. In 1999, *Harry Potter and the Prisoner of Azkaban* appeared, the third installment of Rowling's seven-volume saga of the adventures of a bespectacled boy at a wizard-training school in England. The author's sales had been good before, but this was a publishing event unlike anything since all of London lined up to buy the next installment of *The Pickwick Papers*. Rowling did not so much top the bestseller lists as dominate them. *Harry Potter and the Prisoner of Azkaban* sold a million copies in just a few weeks, at one point outpacing the second-best-selling novel by an astonishing figure of seven to one. It pulled back both its predecessors onto the hardback and the paperback lists, and for two weeks Rowling had, unbelievably, the top three bestselling hardback novels in America *and* the top two paperbacks.

Rowling had literary reasons for her triumph—these were pretty good books—but she had social reasons, as well. Europe and America still have a hunger for the shared topic of conversation that is the main benefit of a middlebrow literary culture. The trashy bestsellerdom of the lowbrow may be shared, but it gives us nothing to talk about. The glossy unbestsellerdom of the highbrow may give us something to talk about, but it isn't shared. Once a middlebrow book reaches a certain number of readers, however, it begins to feed on its success to gain even higher success. Add in the even greater hunger of middle-class parents for their children to have shared literary references, and you have an appetite ravening for something like Harry Potter to feed it.

Along the way, however, Rowling performed another service, for her success wiped clean the picture most readers at the time had of the history of children's literature. That history is usually drawn something along these lines: The Victorians may have invented childhood itself, for the world had never seen anything like those nineteenth-century children before. Regardless, the Victorians at least invented the idea of needing books specifically for children. This meant, of course, that they had no such books to start with, and so, early in the nineteenth century, they pressed into service a number of adult books that have remained in the shared children's canon ever since: *Pilgrim's Progress*, *Don Quixote*, *Gulliver's Travels*, *Robinson Crusoe*, *The Arabian Nights*, and so on.

Some of these were wildly inappropriate. That was the joke when the explorer Richard Burton impishly published a complete translation of *The Arabian Nights* in 1885, proving that the unexpurgated text was far bawdier than the bowdlerized versions everyone knew from their childhood. At one point in *Gulliver's Travels*, Jonathan Swift has his hero stand athwart a road to form a triumphal arch for the Lilliputian army, and publishers of editions for children would always begin by cutting the ribald comments from the miniature soldiers as they passed beneath the giant's tattered trousers.

Still, the pattern remained in place for a long time. *Ivanhoe*, *The Last of the Mohicans*, and *Oliver Twist* were not written for children, although they eventually became identified as children's books. Genre fiction has always had a tendency to slide down the scale from popular adult book to children's classic. Many late Victorian and Edwardian stories made this move from the grown-ups' shelves to the juvenile section—*Twenty Thousand Leagues Under the Sea*, *The Adventures of Sherlock Holmes*, *The Count of Monte Cristo*, *King Solomon's Mines*, *The Prisoner of Zenda*—but the same process was at work as late as *The Lord of the Rings*, published in 1954.

Fairly quickly, however, the Victorians realized they also needed to start writing from scratch the stories they wanted for their children. Many of these books have fallen by the wayside, sometimes fairly (good riddance to Mrs. Molesworth's prim moralizing and W.H.G. Kingston's fatuous adventures) and sometimes unfairly (G.A. Henty's boy histories deserve to be revived). Still, a few of those early and mid-Victorian volumes survive: Hans Christian Anderson's fairy tales, for example, together with *Pinocchio*, *Tom Brown's Schooldays*, and *Alice in Wonderland*.

The real push, however, came with the late Victorians and the Edwardians. Think of all the books from this era that you've read and given as Christmas presents, over and over again: Mark Twain's *The Prince and the Pauper* and Johanna Spyri's *Heidi*. *The Wizard of Oz* and *The Wind in the Willows*. *Peter Pan* and *Anne of Green Gables*. Rudyard Kipling, Beatrix Potter, E. Nesbit, A.A. Milne, Robert Louis Stevenson. This was the golden age of children's books.

A few stray volumes got added in later years. The 1935 *Little House on the Prairie*, for example, though it was set in an earlier time. A sort of silver age is often said to have begun with C.S. Lewis's 1950 *The Lion, the Witch and the Wardrobe* and continued through Sheila Burnford's *The Incredible Journey* in 1961 and Madeleine L'Engle's *A Wrinkle in Time* in 1962. Dr. Seuss found his legs in this era, publishing both *How the Grinch Stole Christmas* and *The Cat in the Hat* in 1957. Three genuinely fine and underrated books arrived in 1956 alone: Dodie Smith's *Hundred and One Dalmatians* (better than the movie versions), Nora Johnson's *The World of Henry Orient* (much better than the movie version), and Gerald Durrell's *My Family and Other Animals*.

Or so the history of children's literature is usually told. That history, however, has proven wrong. J.K. Rowling's success doesn't just give us a recent series to add as an incidental to the received canon. It also gives us a chance to rewrite the entire list of classic children's books we're all supposed to know—for Rowling makes visible the fact that we are actually living *now* in a golden age of children's literature.

One opportunity of this shakeup is the chance to include some older volumes that never quite found the success they deserved as genuinely shared references, the recognizable touchstones of culture. James Agee's 1951 Easter vigil story, *The Morning Watch*, for instance, ought to be a Christian classic, and Paul Horgan's novel of the Southwest, *A Distant Trumpet*, also published in 1951, is a genuinely fine book about the forming of young men. The 1970s and early 1980s were the nadir of children's books in almost everyone's estimation, but Daniel Pinkwater's snarky comedies—think *The Catcher in the Rye*, played for laughs—almost saved those days from the darkness of Judy Blume's resentments. Gary Paulsen's 1987 survival tale *Hatchet* deserved all the prizes it won. David McCord, Jack Prelutsky, and X.J. Kennedy are the best children's poets since Robert Louis Stevenson, Hilaire Belloc, and A.A. Milne (and maybe, in truth, better than those Edwardians).

Another part of the Rowling moment was an opportunity to lose some of the works that are on standard lists of children's books just because they have always been on such lists. *Little Women* is probably here to stay, but can't we cross off *The Wizard of Oz* books? The movie is enough; L. Frank Baum's sloppy fantasy series would find only mockery if it were published today. E. Nesbit remains on the list, I suppose, but she is never quite as good as you expect from the applause *The Wouldbegoods* and *The Railway Children* receive. *Dr. Doolittle* and *Half Magic* and *From the Mixed-Up Files of Mrs. Basil E. Frankweiler* and *Misty of Chincoteague*: These were books that people gave as gifts because there wasn't much that was better being published in their eras. Even Madeleine L'Engle and Beverly Cleary now seem to me to have been overvalued, brackish water praised in the desert of their time.

Mostly, though, Rowling's shakeup of children's literature let us claim the good work written since 1990. Much of it is playful fantasy, such as Gail Carson Levine's fractured fairy tales in *Ella Enchanted*, *The Princess Tales*, and *Fairest*. Diana Wynne Jones wrote her Chrestomanci books from the late 1970s on, but the series laid out many of the paths that other authors would follow, and it continued down to her 2006 volume, *The Pinhoe Egg*. Eva Ibbotson was another older author who was given new life by the revival of fantasy, from her *Secret of Platform 13* in 1994 to her *Island of the Aunts* in 2000.

Neil Gaiman's *Coraline* (2002) and *The Graveyard Book* (2008) are spooky, odd, and serious books for children. Lemony Snicket's thirteen-volume *A Series of Unfortunate Events* may get more of a boost than it deserves from Brett Helquist's illustrations (clearly inspired by Charles Addams), but the books are clever and fun. With Michael Chabon's *Summerland* in 2002, a major adult novelist published an enjoyable if not entirely successful children's story about mythopoeic baseball. Gary Blackwood's historical *The Shakespeare Stealer*, Jean Ferris's comic *Love Among the Walnuts*, Michael Gruber's disturbing *The Witch's Boy*, Cornelia Funke's unexpected *The Thief Lord*, and Eoin Colfer's happily vulgar *Artemis Fowl*. Much of this is sure to last.

Golden ages are not measured by their major figures, since genius comes when it comes, in or out of season. The real advantage of a golden age for a literary genre is the elevation of its second-rank authors. Merely good writers become nearly great writers when they happen to live at the right moment. Few of these recent children's writers (apart from Gaiman and Chabon) are major literary talents, but all of them are better than they would have been in other times.

Want some Christmas presents to give, books drawn from our new canon of children's literature? Start with the Victoriana of Charlotte Yonge's serious *The Daisy Chain* and Lucretia Peabody Hale's comic *Peterkin Papers*. Then move to Gerald Durrell's *My Family and Other Animals* and the poems in X.J. Kennedy's *Brats*. And end with some of the great newer stories: Diana Wynne Jones's *The Lives of Christopher Chant*, for instance, and Neil Gaiman's *Coraline*. Any of them can sit unembarrassed beside *The Wind in the Willows* and *The Just So Stories* and *Treasure Island* and *The Tailor of Gloucester*—all the books we've somehow always known.

Again, however, the question is why so many talented writers would turn away from realism of the *roman* tradition and toward children's literature over the past twenty-five years. Part of the answer is money, of course. There are serious royalties that can come from these books, and J.K. Rowling joined the ranks of the super-rich with the income from her *Harry Potter* series.

But the money is more a sign than a cause of the decline of the novel as the fundamental device by which we seek the psyche in the modern world. Some hunger is clearly being fed by the children's book, something desire for the deep and metaphysical is felt to be present. In children's literature, the possibility of moral judgment, the clear sense of right and wrong, still remains. But even more, children's books still possess a metaphysical clarity about good and evil. And somewhere along the line, the major art-form of the adult novel found itself too thin, too metaphysically barren, to make any similar claim.

V

We could look at science fiction for yet another example, or, for that matter, nearly any other kind of genre fiction in recent years. But perhaps a better way at the question of popular fiction is to think about the old 1950s standby, the middlebrow novel—with Herman Wouk taken as its exemplar.

It is meaningless to say Wouk was a bad writer. He could spin a compelling tale, and he could embroider some serious ideas onto that tale. His prose was clean, and his characters recognizable. Yes, he wasn't Proust. Or Tolstoy. Or Saul Bellow. He was more an ordinary good writer, producing— with *The Caine Mutiny* (1951), for example—solid American middlebrow work better than, say, Sloan Wilson's *The Man in the Gray Flannel Suit* (1955).

That seems fair, doesn't it? The run of 1950s middlebrow classics was so much better than what would later come to claim their spot in American publishing that we forget those books were, by design and reception, resolutely middlebrow. These were not pulp, like L. Sprague de Camp's rewriting of Robert E. Howard's stories for *Tales of Conan*. They were not unabashed thrillers, like Ian Fleming's *Moonraker* or Alistair Maclean's *HMS Ulysses*. They were not exemplars of genre fiction, like Patricia Highsmith's *The Talented Mr. Ripley* or Rex Stout's *Before Midnight*. But neither were they examples of such higher-brow fiction as Nikos Kazantzakis's *The Last Temptation of Christ*, Vladimir Nabokov's *Lolita*, or Graham Greene's *The Quiet American*.

Every one of those books—from *Tales of Conan* to *The Quiet American*—first appeared in 1955, the same year Herman Wouk outsold them all with *Marjorie Morningstar*, his first book after his breakthrough success with his third novel, *The Caine Mutiny*. And both *The Caine Mutiny* and *Marjorie Morningstar* look awfully good compared with later examples of the middlebrow bestseller as Erich Segal's 1970 *Love Story*. Or Robert James Waller's 1992 *The Bridges of Madison County*. Or Charles Frazier's 1997 *Cold Mountain* (a book lavishly praised by the very highbrow critic Alfred Kazin in one of the last reviews he wrote before his death in 1998).

But looking better than *Love Story* is too weak as praise for what Wouk achieved. He wasn't Proust, but he was a damn sight better than Erich Segal. At the time of his death in the spring of 2019, just short of his 105th birthday, Wouk was given the expected outpouring of tributes. In truth, ever since his hundredth birthday, Wouk received accolades and fond ret-rospectives. Partly that's because he seemed a survivor, a living symbol of a different. And partly the acclaim is because, well, Wouk's books really were good middlebrow fare.

Just add it up. From *Don't Stop the Carnival* (1965) to *The Lawgiver* (2012), he proved he was underrated as a comic writer (which shouldn't have been a surprise, given that as a very young man, before the Second World War, he worked as a joke writer for David Freedman and Fred Allen). From *This Is My God* (1959) to *The Will to Live On* (2000), he wrote well-received nonfiction about being Jewish. From *The Winds of War* (1971) to *Inside, Outside* (1985), he showed he could produce the panoramic doorstoppers beloved by readers in the 1970s and 1980s.

Yes, he wrote some clunkers. Wouk was always bitter that his 1948 novel *City Boy* fell unread in the shadow of Norman Mailer's triumph that year with *The Naked and the Dead*, as though readers and book-reviewers had room for only one Jewish author at a time. But the truth is that *City Boy* just wasn't up to the task. Neither, for that matter, was *Youngblood Hawke* (1962), Wouk's peculiar attempt to fictionalize the Southern-boy-comes-to-literary-New-York life of Thomas Wolfe.

In general, though, he could be counted on to write a readable book with some serious ideas in it. Or, perhaps better, a readable book with some serious ideas *on* it, like figures embroidered on a tapestry. In 2013, *Commentary* magazine commissioned an essay by the critic (and highbrow art-historian) Michael J. Lewis, in an effort to undo the "65-year injustice" of *Commentary*'s treatment of the Jewish writer. It wasa wonderful essay, get-ting much right about the man, while walking back the complaint of Nor-man Podhoretz's 1955 review that swatted away *Marjorie Morningstar*, "from its 'indigestible prose' to its simplistic moral analysis."

"That Wouk should pass for a serious writer is perhaps no more an oc-casion of surprise than the success of a dozen other inconsequential novel-ists," Podhoretz wrote. But "the people who enjoy Wouk, I would guess, read him earnestly, with a reverence they never feel when confronted by, say, Thomas B. Costain or Sloan Wilson." Like *The Caine Mutiny*, Pod-horetz explained, *Marjorie Morningstar* "gives its audience a satisfied sense of having grappled with difficult questions"—a world of the old sneer at the middlebrow is contained in that word "satisfied."

Nearly everyone who has written in praise of Wouk in recent years has taken for an example of his depth, his idea-fiction, a scene at the end of *The Caine Mutiny*. The mutineers' Jewish attorney has just won acquittals by setting up Queeg, their despised captain, to look like a neurotic fool on the witness stand. And then, at a bar afterward, the lawyer drunkenly denounces the oh-so-superior young college-boy officers for failing to realize how much they should have supported Queeg. How much they should have understood that it was the old, prewar career-officer mules who kept the Germans from overrunning America and bringing to the New World the Holocaust they had undertaken in Europe.

It's a great scene. A tremendous scene. But Norman Podhoretz was right, all the way back in the 1950s. It's an idea sewn on the story: the picture of a concept, rather than the actual thought. The reversal might have been more plausible—*how could we readers not have realized there was an entirely different way of looking at things?*—if Wouk had allowed Queeg the least moral complexity. No doubt, the captain is wonderfully drawn as a character: memorable in every way, beginning with his name. But an author doesn't get to give us a Dickensian type, and then reverse field in order to flatter readers that they have just had a deep thought. All they have had, in truth, is the picture of a thought: a simulacrum of ideas, unearned by the prose.

Which is perfectly fine for a certain kind of fiction. This might almost be the definition, the archetype, of the middlebrow. And something like Wouk's *War and Remembrance* (1978) is almost always more enjoyable to read than books like, say, Graham Greene's *The Quiet American*. In fact, *The Caine Mutiny* is better of its middlebrow kind than *The Quiet American* is of its more highbrow kind. But the point is that they're different types of books, built with different ambitions and aimed at different audiences. And the error we make—the error made by too much of the recent praise for Wouk—comes from confusing the two.

Still, all in all, Herman Wouk was a good writer who wrote good books, a few of which are genuinely memorable middlebrow classics. He wasn't Marcel Proust, but he wasn't Thomas B. Costain either. That seems fair, doesn't it?

The middlebrow, in other words, is a kind of novel. A type, a genre. And the sneer at it from higher precincts is almost always accompanied by a sense, unearned and far too easy, of superiority in the readers capable of understanding the complexities that the grand novel of high ambition could convey. In retrospect, judging by what came after, *The Caine Mutiny* and other middlebrow classics of the 1950s stand clearly as a type of the general novel that had been building since Defore published *Robinson Crusoe*.

Compare the novel to, say, the Charles Frazier's *Cold Mountain*—the literary triumph of 1997. At the peak of its success, one was hard pressed to avoid knowing everything about *Cold Mountain*. The book sold something like a million copies in hard cover, clung to the *New York Times* best-seller list for twenty-six weeks, was snatched up by Hollywood for $1.25 million, and received a surprising National Book Award (beating out Don DeLillo's heavily favored *Underworld*). Over a thousand pieces about Frazier's novel appeared in American newspapers and magazines, until reviewers were at last reduced to telling more about the story *of* the book than about the story *in* the book.

But there is, of course, a story in the book. In Frazier's lightweight version of Homer's *Odyssey*, it's a Civil War tale of a soldier named Inman who wakes up one 1864 morning in a field hospital of the Confederate Army of Northern Virginia and reckons that since the war is pretty much lost, he'd best get on back to Miss Ada, the good woman waiting for him back on a farm way up in the hills and hollers.

Along his road home, Inman spends considerable time recollecting his childhood—especially the teachings he received from the last of the Cherokees—and has his quota of adventures: rescuing imperiled women and children, travelling beside a lapsed preacher, dodging the Home Guard rounding up "outliers" for the last futile war effort, and narrowly escaping three alluring harpies looking either to kill him or marry him, or maybe both.

And meanwhile, in alternating chapters, Miss Ada is having her own share of adventures. The daughter of an Emerson-and-water sort of Protestant minister who came from an upper-class Charleston home to preach in the wilds of the Blue Ridge mountains, Ada is hard pressed to keep the family farm going after her father's death. What she'd like most to do is wander the fields in spring sketching the flowers, reading George Eliot, and remembering the snubs she gave all the young men besides Inman who came to court and spark. Only she's starving to death doing it—Frazier is convincing at the details of the inflationary Confederate economy toward the end of the war—and it's not till a ragamuffin farm girl named Ruby shows up to help that the long wait for Inman becomes bearable.

Ruby is the daughter of an itinerant fiddler, a man who reappears occasionally to make life difficult (although one time he brings along, so everyone can pair off nicely at the novel's end, a young deserter just right for a hard-headed woman like Ruby to transform from no-account trash into a man of substance). Between the two of them, the manless women Ada and Ruby manfully improve the farm, flourish in the small towns' barter markets, and braid one another's womanly hair by the evening firelight.

From its opening among the dying and the sightless in an army hospital, however, the novel has promised a tragic ending. Even as Inman nears Ada and home, the lawless Home Guard has drawn closer and closer. Though the hero manages to kill all the worst ones, they at last shoot him down and he dies—but not before he has one night of passion with Ada. *Cold Mountain* ends with a picture, a few years down the road, of Ruby and her shaped-up husband still living on the farm. And Miss Ada? She watches at play the daughter of her night with her returned Odysseus and muses with a sad smile how (in one last salvo from the novel's barrage of classical reference) she and Inman just never had a chance to grow old together and turn into trees like Baucis and Philemon.

In the acknowledgements at the back of the book, where he explains that he drew his story from the genuine adventures of a Confederate ancestor, Frazier gives his hero's name as W.P. Inman. In the novel itself, however, the character is just plain "Inman," the absence of a Christian name suggesting—well, suggesting for Frazier all sorts of much too simplistic things: that Inman is the in-man, for instance, inside all kinds of secrets that most folks just wrap themselves around the outside of. Remember how, in Jack Schaefer's classic 1949 a-stranger-came-to-town tale *Shane*, the hero had just that one name, and nobody could figure out whether it was his first or his last? Well, in *Cold Mountain*, Inman's lack of a Christian name is supposed to give him the same whiff of the mysterious while simultaneously hinting that Inman, though he may like to tell a story or two from time to time, is really the strong, silent type whose rich inner life is shielded from the prying and prattle of flashy outer men.

But it's far too easy to apply this sort of mocking literary criticism to *Cold Mountain*—too easy and too unfair, the result of shining much too bright a light on the book. Charles Frazier had his pretensions, no doubt: the kind, for instance, that caused him to describe himself as a horse-breeder, leaving off his author biography the fact that he taught literature. Pretending that he has no literary pretensions (even while producing a book that owes plenty to unreflective literary convention), Frazier studs his novel with allusions to the Greek classics to make sure *nobody* misses that he's retelling the *Odyssey*.

All that's no reason we have to share the author's pretensions, however, and in its own league, *Cold Mountain* is actually quite good. Nonetheless, a critical backlash set in against the book toward the end of 1997. At its first publication in June, Frazier's novel received the generally mild reviews typically accorded publishers' mid-list books and found the small regional success in the South that Atlantic Monthly Press doubtless had as its highest aspiration. *Cold Mountain*, however, never quite made its expected drift off to the remainder bins. One reader kept telling another to read it, George Will used his widely syndicated political column to applaud it, and a national fever for the novel took hold.

As long as bestsellers are pure pulp in the class of Harold Robbins's 1961 *The Carpetbaggers* (better than you think) and Jacqueline Susann's 1966 *The Valley of the Dolls* (worse than you remember), reviewers usually ignore them or write only about the decadent pleasures of slumming down in them. And as long as semi-literary historical novels don't top the sales charts, reviewers usually praise them faintly. But super-bestsellerdom, when combined with enough bookishness to make average readers imagine that they've just read a piece of serious literature, seems to bring out the sternest instincts of critics: Highbrow is fine, and lowbrow is fun, but the successful middlebrow must be swatted down.

So *National Review* (in a generally sympathetic essay) derided Frazier for sounding "the way novelists sound when they sound like novelists." The *Washington Times* (in an utterly dismissive column) snorted that Inman is "not your average Confederate soldier, you see. He's an Indian medicine man with all the latest Indian styles from Haight-Ashbury." The *New York Times*, *Washington Post*, and *Los Angeles Times* all left the book off their year-end round-ups of the best fiction of 1997. Noticing its lack of quotation marks, thinned-down prose, and backwoods setting, *Kirkus Reviews* called *Cold Mountain* "refried Cormac McCarthy"—which is fair, so long as one remembers that McCarthy, tired of selling only a few dozen copies of books that critics compared to William Faulkner's, had already refried himself to produce his 1992 bestseller, *All the Pretty Horses*.

Like an engineering expert brought in to look over a home-repair project, any well-trained critic who examines the book too closely is bound to find the flaws in *Cold Mountain*: bumpy joints, rickety framing, exposed wiring, maybe even that Frazier added a second story to his novel and forgot to build a stairway to it. Writing for the on-line journal *Slate*, the *New Republic*'s fiction critic James Wood was exactly right to notice the novel's "writing-school style," "literary approximation of an already literary idea of reality," and creaky alternation of Penelope/Odysseus chapters about Ada and Inman: "She waits; he travels." Wood, however, was exactly wrong to conclude that *Cold Mountain* "is like a cemetery with no bodies in it." Who breaks a butterfly upon a wheel?

In fact, hardly anyone got *Cold Mountain* quite right at the time. Frazier produced a perfectly enjoyable piece of sentimental fiction, straight from those golden days of the 1950s when there flourished in America such guardians of middlebrow taste as Clifton Fadiman, *Reader's Digest* Condensed Books, and the Book-of-the-Month Club. In the careful design of its almost blueprinted sentimentality, *Cold Mountain* betrays some serious cold-bloodedness. But then *Love Story* betrayed even more—as did, for that matter, such middlebrow classics as *Shane* and Edwin O'Connor's *The Last Hurrah*. (It may be the most devastating criticism of *The Bridges of Madison County* to suggest that its author *wasn't* being cold-blooded, but actually meant it.)

Of course, for all his 1950s-style middlebrow success, Frazier puts in his novel plenty of uniquely 1990s-style asides. At one point, *Cold Mountain* makes a smug little gesture at female masturbation, and the book is capable of the historical tone of describing "dipped Baptists" on one page and the historical tone-deafness of calling Christ's Resurrection "his culture's central narrative" on the page before. The novelist is good when his characters describe war, but terrible when they theorize about it: dismissing as equally "despots" the northern soldiers and the southern slaveholders, and accusing Robert E. Lee, of all people, of thinking that military might makes moral right. With his brave deserter, Frazier gets to have it both ways: Inman fleeing defeat is somehow the same as Odysseus returning from victory. The Civil War is almost over anyway, and Inman has merely decided in his ahistorical way to make a separate peace—and just in case anyone might think him a coward, the author has him kill three Yankee raiders who must deserve killing because they've threatened a sickly little baby and brave little woman that Inman met along the road.

And yet, even if Frazier is untrustworthy on women, religion, and war—even if he is willing to violate his novel's historical accuracy for the sake of saying the socially correct thing about them—the question remains. So what? What novelist of the late twentieth century *was* entirely trustworthy on women, religion, and war? If there's any clue in the way he keeps stepping on his retelling of the *Odyssey*—hiding it behind long descriptions of made-up Cherokee spirituality and woodsman's lore—then Frazier probably didn't much care about his own classic, mythopoeic story. What he probably intended readers to take away from his book is his heroines' spunky proto-feminism and all his New Age nonsense about the hundred-year-old Indian goat woman and his hero's will to fight no more forever.

What authors intend for their books, however, is not what matters. Arthur Conan Doyle hated his creation, Sherlock Holmes, first trying to kill him off and then transmuting him into a seamless opsimath who knows everything from medieval music to the inner lives of bees (when, in the early stories, Holmes didn't even know that the earth moves around the sun). None of it managed to destroy his character. Doyle's Sherlock Holmes may not belong in the same class as Shakespeare's Hamlet or Dickens's Pickwick, any more than Frazier's Inman actually ranges near Homer's Odysseus. But Inman manages nonetheless to gesture at the mythopoeic.

Which is what the middlebrow is supposed to do. *Cold Mountain* is less intelligent than *The Caine Mutiny*, but it wanted to be a throwback to the era of Herman Wouk's kind of book—and it is worth asking why, for that ambition reveals the novel's superiority to Erich Segal's *Love Story* or Robert James Waller's *The Bridges of Madison County*.

The answer proves interestingly parallel to the conclusions drawn when we considered the boom of graphic novels and children's literature in recent decades. The standard art-form of the novel appeared to be failing us. It no longer told us what we are. It no longer explained the way we live now.

Only by reaching back to a more coherent world could right and wrong be made to stand out clearly. The 1950s were much mocked at the time, its culture sneered at as middlebrow. But in retrospect it would come to seem like something of a golden age for writers, giving them that for which Charles Frazier's hungered in *Cold Mountain*: a clarity about the reality of good and evil that escaped the thinness and metaphysical barrenness under which more recent novels suffered.

CHAPTER 10 | CONCLUSION

It's been almost fifty years since Shūsaku Endō published *Silence*, the book I am regularly tempted to call the best novel of the second half of the twentieth century. At least, it is the book whose impact, when I first read it, still provides the benchmark by which I judge the ambition and the success of contemporary novels—of every new work I've read in the twenty years since.

Of the authors who have published novels since the early 1990s, none are mandatory reading. Or, at least, none are mandatory within a certain understanding of culture and art in our day—which is, of course, the problem we have been tracing. And as this study has tried to show, the lack of cultural centrality is not necessarily the authors' fault. We just don't read novels the way we used to. We have no one who occupies the position of, say, Saul Bellow—in part because his talents flourished at a time in which there was still an identifiable cultural space for them. Where now is that kind of space? The great ambitions have dwindled, and the engine of the art form sputters on the last fumes of its old fuel. Modernity's metaphysical crisis of the thick self in a thin world was not solved, by the novel or anything else. And, in consequence, we have been overtaken by a second crisis, a crisis debilitating for art, as the culture loses its horizons and its sense of purpose.

That hardly means no fiction has been attempted over the past half century. From V.S. Naipaul, Mario Vargas Llosa, Thomas Pynchon, Philip Roth, and Don DeLillo (all five born in the 1930s) to such figures as J.M. Coetzee and John Irving (both born in the early 1940s), there have always been authors who remember the novel's ambitions. For decades, serious readers of novels would snatch up anything new by Martin Amis, Salman Rushdie, and Cormac McCarthy, simply as a matter of course. I am not a great admirer of the work of Ian McEwan and Jonathan Franzen—the way I am enthusiastic about anything by Marilynne Robinson, A.S. Byatt, and Michael Chabon—but they all need to be read if one follows contemporary fiction. Add in such writers as Zadie Smith, Haruki Murakami, Orhan Pamuk, Arundhati Roy, Jeffrey Eugenides, a dozen others, and we have a fairly standard list, a kind of newspapery report, of applauded writers of contemporary fiction of a relatively high and serious kind.

And yet, immensely talented as they are, we can still ask why none of them seems to tower in our sense of the novel, the way the foundational English authors do, from Daniel Defoe to Jane Austen. Or the way the High Victorians do, from Dickens and Thackeray to Henry James. Or the way the Modernists do, from Proust and Joyce to Thomas Mann and Ralph Ellison. Or even the mid-twentieth-century novelists do, from Fitzgerald, Faulkner, and Hemingway to Sinclair Lewis and John Steinbeck. In these pages, we have not sorted through much contemporary fiction, in large part because we haven't needed to. The history of the novel has made their project tenuous, and Jane Austen herself could not entirely restore it.

We might make the same point by contemplating, as we did in the last chapter, the golden age of genre fiction through which we are living. Most self-consciously literaturized genre fiction fails; Thomas Pynchon's genre books, for example, have been less ambitious than his earlier work. (Although we should mention *Jonathan Strange and Mr. Norrell*, Susanna Clarke's utterly enjoyable if overlong 2004 pastiche of eighteenth-century prose in service of a Randall Garrett-like alternate history in which magic survives into the time of the Napoleonic Wars.) But the greatest of the contemporary genre writers, the ones who have embraced their forms and dwell happily within them, have produced the fiction that the culture actually reads and remembers.

Neil Gaiman is a genius of his kind, exploring genre fiction in children's books, urban fantasy, and graphic novels. Dean Koontz used horror, in ways I suspect much of his enormous audience does not realize, precisely to raise metaphysical questions about the world's disenchantment. George R.R. Martin's *Game of Thrones* success is a model of rich world construction in the post-J.R.R. Tolkien age, while Gene Wolfe used science fiction to undertake a Catholic-tinged literary project for over thirty years. A dozen others could easily be named here, starting with the two bestselling authors since Agatha Christie: Stephen King and J.K. Rowling. And then there are all the authors and artists involved in the maturing of the comic book into the graphic novel: the superhero revisionists Alan Moore and Frank Miller, for example; Chris Ware with *Jimmy Corrigan*, Art Spiegelman with *Maus*, Marjane Satrapi with *Persepolis*.

They are all talented writers, but again, the very fact of their talent raises a question—in this case, the question of why they bother with genre fiction. To see someone elevate a police-procedural mystery or a comic book to higher levels of art is to wonder why they aren't writing ambitious novels, working in the artistic form the culture had spent almost three hundred years developing into a device of extraordinary subtlety, range, and power. To see a great ukulele player is to wonder why someone with talent enough to play the ukulele well is playing the ukulele.

In our recoil from the snobbery of the question, the question finds its answer. Robert Heinlein with his science fiction, P.G. Wodehouse with his romantic comedies, and Rex Stout with his mysteries would not have minded the suggestion that perhaps they were not working at the level of the Nobel-prizewinning Thomas Mann, although all three published books in 1947, the same year Mann's *Doctor Faustus* appeared, and all three were masters of their particular genres and fixtures (especially Wodehouse) in the literary landscape. When we sense now something elitist and conde-scending in the distinction between "serious fiction" and "genre fiction," we are actually revealing that we don't believe in the power of the old forms of serious fiction—a disbelief that would not have been shared by even the best of genre writers in previous generations, from Arthur Conan Doyle to Dr. Seuss.

And that, precisely, is what is we ought to understand by the idea of the decline of the novel. It is not a claim that greater genius existed in pre-vious centuries, or a claim that genius is wasting itself in popular art. It is, rather, a claim that the great purpose of the modern novel was to re-enchant our sense of the world with fictional narratives that put in parallel the sanc-tifying journey of the soul with the physical and social journey of the body. That purpose was, to phrase it another way, to knit back together the inte-rior and exterior realities that the modern age had split apart. And as West-ern culture stumbles along, head down, no longer confident that modernity *can* be solved, the old project seems slightly unreal. So what ought we do for an art? What ought we to do with ourselves?

AFTERWORD

I am such a slow writer that, even to complete this small work, I had to go back to previous essays and reviews, borrowing sentences, paragraphs, and even whole sections from work I'd previously published in *Nineteenth-Century Literature*, the *Wall Street Journal*, the *Weekly Standard*, *Books & Culture*, the *Free Beacon*, and other journals. To the editors of all these publications, especially to John Wilson, I owe enormous thanks.

I must thank as well Brian Murray of Loyola University in Baltimore, a friend who contributed greatly to my discussion of Walter Scott, and the New York writer David Goldman, who gently corrected my misapprehensions of German literature as I worked out my enthusiasm for Thomas Mann. My wife Lorena and daughter Faith allowed me to disappear into my study and finish, at last, this small account of the novel. Innumerable discussions of novels over the years with Margaret Boerner formed my thinking far more than any college class ever did.

It's only when I undertake projects like this, broad intellectual endeavors, that I feel a twinge of regret that I live out here in on the edge of a western forest in South Dakota, a thousand miles from conversation with many friends. But in another way, that distance itself is what has allowed me the space to muster my thoughts about the novel and the time to write those thoughts down.

The Black Hills
September 2019

4✓

3–, 9, 11–12, 15, 18

23–26, 30, 34

–35✓   41

43✓ – 44 47 48✓ 60, 69 70

92– 93, 94   98–99–101

116–117✓ – 118

128– 129✓ – 130, 134, 137,

138–139✓, 149 – 152